Cambridge Elements ≡

Elements in Global China
edited by
Ching Kwan Lee
University of California

CHINESE GLOBAL INFRASTRUCTURE

Austin Strange
The University of Hong Kong

CAMBRIDGE
UNIVERSITY PRESS

Shaftesbury Road, Cambridge CB2 8EA, United Kingdom

One Liberty Plaza, 20th Floor, New York, NY 10006, USA

477 Williamstown Road, Port Melbourne, VIC 3207, Australia

314–321, 3rd Floor, Plot 3, Splendor Forum, Jasola District Centre, New Delhi – 110025, India

103 Penang Road, #05–06/07, Visioncrest Commercial, Singapore 238467

Cambridge University Press is part of Cambridge University Press & Assessment, a department of the University of Cambridge.

We share the University's mission to contribute to society through the pursuit of education, learning and research at the highest international levels of excellence.

www.cambridge.org
Information on this title: www.cambridge.org/9781009486910

DOI: 10.1017/9781009090902

First published 2023

A catalogue record for this publication is available from the British Library

ISBN 978-1-009-48691-0 Hardback
ISBN 978-1-009-08834-3 Paperback
ISSN 2632-7341 (online)
ISSN 2632-7333 (print)

Additional resources for this publication at www.cambridge.org/ 9781009486910

Chinese Global Infrastructure

Elements in Global China

DOI: 10.1017/9781009090902
First published online: November 2023

Austin Strange
The University of Hong Kong
Author for correspondence: Austin Strange, astrange@hku.hk

Abstract: Infrastructure is at the heart of China's presence in global development and is also central to larger debates about Chinese influence. This Element provides a comprehensive account of major Chinese government-financed infrastructure projects in the Global South since 1949. Using new datasets, it demonstrates that Chinese global infrastructure is distinct in terms of its historical tenacity and massive contemporary scope. But this does not imply that contemporary Chinese global infrastructure or the Belt and Road Initiative should be studied in a vacuum. Historical and comparative perspectives show that contemporary projects often emerge based on similar political logics to those that shaped infrastructure investment in earlier periods of Chinese history and other international contexts. The Element then examines how infrastructure projects have created both purposeful and unintended sources of influence by serving as valuable but risky political capital for host country governments as well as the Chinese government.

Keywords: China, infrastructure, development finance, international development, international relations

ISBNs: 9781009486910 (HB), 9781009088343 (PB), 9781009090902 (OC)
ISSNs: 2632-7341 (online), 2632-7333 (print)

Contents

1 Questions about Infrastructure and Influence

Infrastructure is central to China's reemergence in global development since the late 1990s. Around that time, the Chinese government began financing overseas development projects at a breathtaking pace. Since 2000, it has committed hundreds of billions of dollars for projects in transportation, energy, industry, water, and other infrastructure-heavy sectors. The Belt and Road Initiative (BRI), launched in 2013 to promote connectivity along a broadly envisaged overland "belt" in Eurasia and a maritime "road" spanning several regions, accelerated this trend, and China soon became the largest bilateral provider of development finance in the Global South (Dreher et al. 2022). Today, physical infrastructures such as roads, highways, railroads, bridges, ports, dams, power plants, factories, mines, pipelines, stadiums, government buildings, and event venues visually embody China's massive, complicated role as a provider of development capital.

China's global infrastructure spree has attracted widespread international attention, particularly in the United States and other liberal democracies concerned about China's growing economic power, as well as in developing countries that host Chinese-financed projects. Debates are contentious and often polarized. Advocates appreciate the speed, efficiency, and lack of bureaucratic red tape with which China finances and builds development "hardware" (Wade 2008; Shikwati, Adero, and Juma 2022). Critics warn that China is a strategic, opaque lender determined to extract natural resources and policy concessions while making recipient countries less prosperous, more debt-laden, and less democratic (Naim 2007; Chellaney 2017). Other skeptics contend that Chinese infrastructure is economically wasteful, consisting of "useless buildings" and roads to nowhere.[1] The BRI's first decade has intensified this debate by providing opportunities for enthusiasts and skeptics alike to gather anecdotes as datapoints for their respective claims.

Concerns about Chinese overseas infrastructure in particular have fueled larger assertions about China's global economic influence. Outside suspicion toward Chinese overseas infrastructure projects is of course not new, much less did it originate with the BRI. For example, the "rogue aid" label first popularized by *Foreign Policy* in 2007 suggested that China offers aid and infrastructure abroad for "boosting international alliances that advance China's *growing global influence*" (Naim 2007, 97; emphasis added). Decades earlier, Cold War–era Chinese global infrastructure projects were similarly criticized by Western observers as tools of an expansionist foreign policy designed to accumulate influence and spread political ideology (Large 2008).

---

[1] www.abc.net.au/news/2018-01-10/australia-hits-out-at-chinese-aid-to-pacific/9316732.

Today, such sentiments are even stronger. According to some accounts, China's influence is advancing in lockstep with its economic development. The US Department of State is publicly operating on this assumption, asserting in 2020 that China's "global reach and international influence have expanded accordingly" following four decades of rapid growth (Office of the Secretary of State 2020, 40). Chinese global infrastructure is often seen as an important influence tool within this narrative. Observers have suggested that China is "weaponizing" the BRI to bring other countries into its orbit (Russel and Berger 2020). In particular, the opaqueness of Chinese policy bank-issued loans for infrastructure creates potential for massive liabilities, including "hidden debt" that China might shield from the international community and wield as a "debt trap" to exercise influence over other countries (Chellaney 2017; Gelpern et al. 2022).

This viewpoint has been popular in the corridors of power within the United States amid mounting bilateral tensions. The US 2017 National Security Strategy asserts that "China's infrastructure investment and trade strategies reinforce its geopolitical aspirations" (Trump 2017). In 2018 Vice President Mike Pence contended that "China uses so-called 'debt diplomacy' to expand its influence," and that for China's development finance to developing countries, "the benefits invariably flow overwhelmingly to Beijing" (Pence 2018). A year later, former Secretary of State Mike Pompeo criticized Beijing for brokering "corrupt infrastructure deals in exchange for political influence."[2] In 2021, Secretary of State Antony Blinken suggested that many BRI host countries "feel pressured to take bad deals on terms set by others," tacitly referring to China's influence over these governments.[3]

American anxieties about the consequences of Chinese global infrastructure are shared by other governments. French President Emmanuel Macron stated in 2018 that new Silk Roads built along the BRI are "a tool to promote new international standards, rules and norms."[4] The same year, Penny Wong, now Australia's Minister of Foreign Affairs, remarked that the BRI "is a game-changer" that "employs economic power as an expression of strategic power" and represents "a fundamental change in the way that strategic business is done."[5] Host country governments have also occasionally perceived Chinese infrastructure projects as influence conduits. As discussed in Section 4, former

---

[2] www.theguardian.com/technology/2019/may/08/mike-pompeo-invokes-thatcher-push-harder-line-china-huawei.

[3] www.state.gov/a-free-and-open-indo-pacific/.

[4] www.reuters.com/article/us-china-france-idUSKBN1EX0FU.

[5] www.smh.com.au/politics/federal/chinas-massive-global-infrastructure-spending-a-game-chan ger-for-world-power-says-labors-penny-wong-20180123-h0n09g.html.

Malaysian Prime Minister Mahathir Mohamad in 2018 criticized "unfair" infrastructure deals signed by his predecessor that would disproportionately benefit China and leave Malaysia "indebted," and later advised other infrastructure-seeking countries to "regulate or limit influences from China."[6]

Concerned governments have begun backing rhetoric with bilateral and multilateral policy responses. Both the United States and Japan have notably eschewed the Asian Infrastructure Investment Bank (AIIB), a Chinese-led multilateral, infrastructure-focused development bank founded in 2015. In 2018, the US Congress passed the Better Utilization of Investments Leading to Development (BUILD) Act, which enabled the formation of the Development Finance Corporation designed in part to finance infrastructure alternatives to Chinese-financed projects. In November 2019, Australia, Japan, and the United States launched the "Blue Dot Network" to monitor the quality of global infrastructure projects, including those financed and built by China. In December 2021 the European Union (EU) established the Global Gateway and in June 2022 the Group of Seven (G7) unveiled the Partnership for Global Infrastructure Investment (PGII), formerly Build Back Better World (B3W), ostensibly to provide alternative infrastructure initiatives to the BRI. The United States claims that PGII will deliver "game-changing projects to close the infrastructure gap in developing countries, strengthen the global economy and supply chains, and advance U.S. national security."[7]

Researchers have been more cautious in questioning and qualifying assertions about Chinese infrastructure and influence. But policy and popular debates have largely abandoned nuance and clarity in favor of a linear narrative that pegs China's influence to its global infrastructure and other investments, even as many observers possess strong doubts about the economic viability and future of the BRI. This has primed audiences to fixate on the potential influence benefits of infrastructure for China while downplaying its potential risks.

Moreover, despite enormous policy, media, and academic interest, the conceptual and empirical contours of Chinese global infrastructure remain surprisingly unclear. A large literature has unpacked the nature and impacts of different forms of Chinese overseas development capital (e.g. Alden 2007; Bräutigam 2009; Lee 2017; Dreher et al. 2022). But there are few if any systematic accounts of Chinese overseas infrastructure, which instead is often bundled into more general studies of Chinese aid, lending, and investment. Moreover, existing measures of infrastructure often rely on indirect measures of financial

---

[6] www.reuters.com/article/uk-china-malaysia-trade-idUKKCN1L5072; www.straitstimes.com/asia/se-asia/beware-of-china-debt-trap-malaysias-mahathir-tells-the-philippines.

[7] www.whitehouse.gov/briefing-room/statements-releases/2022/06/26/fact-sheet-president-biden-and-g7-leaders-formally-launch-the-partnership-for-global-infrastructure-and-investment/.

flows rather than actual infrastructure projects. For example, researchers employing statistical analyses often proxy for infrastructure by aggregating dollars committed to infrastructure-intensive sectors such as energy, transport, and industry, or to financial flow types such as loans, lines of credit, export buyer's and seller's credits, and other instruments (e.g. Blair, Marty, and Roessler 2022; Zeitz 2021; Dreher et al. 2022). Qualitative research that employs interviews, case studies, site visits, or other approaches has carefully examined many individual Chinese-supported infrastructure projects around the world, but struggles to generate scalable, systematic inferences due to local contextual factors.

In addition, existing accounts of the BRI and Chinese overseas infrastructure offer remarkably little comparative or historical context for their claims. This recency bias discounts both earlier eras of Chinese global infrastructure and preexisting knowledge from other fields about domestic and international infrastructure projects. It also makes it difficult to assess whether and how contemporary Chinese global infrastructure is distinctive in its motives, features, and impacts.

China's "infrastructure-influence nexus," that is, the ways in which infrastructure potentially generates influence, remains similarly nebulous despite immense curiosity. Many existing accounts assume that infrastructure creates Chinese influence but do not specify how this occurs.[8] Most research has focused on high-level policy outcomes, such as China's ability to finance and build infrastructure in exchange for diplomatic and political support by other governments, though evidence suggests that rising powers like China also care deeply about "winning hearts and minds" among foreign public audiences (e.g. Brazys and Dukalskis 2019). In general, few studies have rigorously considered how infrastructure in particular might generate influence for China's government (e.g. Hillman 2019a; Ho 2020).

In short, the BRI has attracted immense public and scholarly attention as a global infrastructure drive since its launch a decade ago. But despite this curiosity, we have surprisingly little clarity about what Chinese global infrastructure actually refers to, or how it impacts China's pursuit of international influence.

This Element offers a comprehensive account of Chinese global infrastructure and helps address the aforementioned questions in three steps. First, it

---

[8] This is symptomatic of a larger challenge of measuring how China's growing material resources translate into influence. Other work shows that Chinese trade, investment, and aid are important influence conduits (e.g. Kastner 2016; Norris 2016; Dreher et al. 2018). Other scholars have considered various other conditions under which China can influence developing countries (e.g. Goh 2014; Lampton, Ho, and Kuik 2020).

situates China's twenty-first-century global infrastructure drive within China's broader global development finance program since 1949. It offers a general definition of Chinese global infrastructure that can be applied to study a wide range of China's most economically and politically consequential infrastructure projects in the Global South. In particular, it spotlights two primary forms of global infrastructure that China has consistently financed and built: "high-profile" infrastructure such as transportation and other large, economically productive projects, and nationally symbolic "prestige" infrastructure such as government buildings and stadiums.

Second, it operationalizes this definition and employs two newly created datasets to directly measure Chinese global infrastructure projects committed since 1949. One of these datasets was constructed over the past three years, during which my research team catalogued approximately 4,000 total projects, including nearly 1,500 physical infrastructure projects, that the Chinese government committed to developing countries during the second half of the twentieth century. This comprehensive catalog of historical projects challenges overwhelmingly present-focused accounts of Chinese global infrastructure. Decades before the BRI was conceived, the Chinese government had already begun financing and building global infrastructure at scale, including hundreds of high-profile and prestige projects in over 100 countries across Africa, Asia, and other developing regions.

Third, the Element helps clarify how global infrastructure generates different intended and unintended influence outcomes that affect China's interests. Chinese global infrastructure is a valuable form of national political capital for host country leaders who can acquire and brand projects to serve a variety of economic and political functions. But China's overseas infrastructure projects are no less immune to well-known pitfalls that have jeopardized other large-scale infrastructure ventures throughout history. The same features that make infrastructure attractive also tend to make its planners prone to risk miscalculation. In addition to economic risks, earlier Chinese global infrastructure and the BRI have demonstrated that overseas infrastructure can also introduce major volatility for states' international influence, even when influence-seeking is not the primary objective. These projects have unpredictable trajectories and have likely complicated rather than enhanced China's global influence, and have also diminished the ability of the Chinese government to control its net influence abroad. Overall, global infrastructure has been a useful tool for China's pursuit of high-level influence outcomes such as political support from foreign governments. But its returns for China's popular influence and image abroad, as well as China's longer-term net influence, are considerably murkier.

Important takeaways emerge from this contextual approach. Contemporary Chinese global infrastructure is unique in terms of its currently unrivalled scale throughout the Global South. The evidence presented below shows that China is also rather distinct in terms of its consistent willingness to provide global infrastructure since the Cold War. But historical and comparative perspectives also reveal that contemporary Chinese global infrastructure projects are hardly exceptional. Their political dynamics often resemble those of earlier Chinese-financed global infrastructure, and of other large infrastructure ventures pursued by governments and other stakeholders in a variety of settings.

Moreover, Chinese global infrastructure projects remain as much *political ventures* as they are *financial investments*. Overlapping domestic and international political incentives between host country governments and China's government provide important rationale for both sides to pursue global infrastructure. These visible, nationally relevant projects promise short-term political benefits – including potential influence for China's government – but also generate major economic and political uncertainty for governments over time. More careful appreciation for global infrastructure's political dynamics complements recent research heavily focused on the financing and debt aspects of Chinese infrastructure lending. Chinese global infrastructure's political logic is crucial for understanding its long-term persistence in developing countries.

The remainder of the Element proceeds as follows. Section 2 provides a primer on the evolution of China's development finance from 1949 in order to situate contemporary Chinese global infrastructure. It explains how China's government arrived at its current position as the world's largest provider of global infrastructure, and how important policy foundations were laid down during the second half of the twentieth century. It also synthesizes a large literature on the nature, motives, and consequences of Chinese development finance – including but not limited to infrastructure – that has emerged over the past 20 years.

Section 3 turns specifically to Chinese overseas infrastructure development projects. A sprawling, interdisciplinary literature suggests that these projects generate important short-term economic benefits as well as longer-term risks. I introduce the concept of "global infrastructure," defined as government-financed physical infrastructure projects which are both highly visible and nationally salient in other countries. I focus on two prominent forms of Chinese global infrastructure: "High-profile" projects are large-scale, complex economic infrastructure projects, including massive transportation, energy, and other productive infrastructures. "Prestige" projects are financially smaller but equally visible and flashy infrastructure projects possessing national symbolism such as government buildings, stadiums, and conference centers, and are primarily allocated to small states in the Global South. Global infrastructure's visibility and national scope produces an outsized, conspicuous presence that host country politicians amplify through their own branding efforts. These features make global infrastructure distinct forms of political capital for both host country governments and China's government relative to other types of development cooperation. Section 3 utilizes two new datasets to document China's provision of global infrastructure since 1949.

Section 4 turns to the relationship between infrastructure and influence. It argues that global infrastructure possesses outsized scale, complexity, and visibility that magnify both its political benefits for host country governments and influence possibilities for donor and lender governments. In the short-term, global infrastructure offers concrete political capital for both host country leaders and for China's government. The former can seek, acquire, and brand high-profile or prestige infrastructure as national achievements that serve a variety of domestic political purposes, while China's government can provide these projects to enhance its international influence. These features make global infrastructure politically attractive for governments in the short term, but also create complicated and poorly understood political consequences for China's government and host country governments as projects move from conception to reality. In particular, global infrastructure activates unintended "influence externalities" for China via political mobilization and infrastructure narratives in host countries that muddle the net political value of these projects and weaken governments' control over influence outcomes.

Section 5 summarizes and reflects on the Element's main findings. It concludes that the BRI is an important chapter in a larger history of Chinese global infrastructure and in a much larger, global story of states' consistent attraction to infrastructure despite massive socioeconomic and political risks. This broader view helps grasp the roles of political in addition to economic considerations that lead host countries and the Chinese government to jointly pursue global infrastructure. It also suggests that global infrastructure is likely to remain as a central component of China's development cooperation even as it evolves into digital and other new forms with different stakeholders and financial arrangements.

2 The Lineage of Chinese Overseas Development Projects

How did China's government become the world's largest provider of infrastructure in developing countries? This section first provides a background of China's broader set of global development activities since 1949 to situate Chinese global infrastructure. It reviews evidence on the motives and impacts of China's global development projects and then discusses two new datasets that can be used to document and analyze Chinese global infrastructure.

2.1 China's Long March toward Global Infrastructure

Policymakers, journalists, and scholars have closely scrutinized the growing overseas development programs of China and other "emerging donors" since 2000 (Woods 2008). But China is not a new donor or creditor. The People's Republic of China (PRC) initiated overseas development assistance almost immediately after its founding in 1949. Since then, China's basic posture toward overseas development finance has shifted multiple times, often in response to changing political and economic priorities at home. For example, China was a net donor throughout most of the Mao era. Outgoing aid was an important foreign policy tool driven heavily by political and ideological directives, particularly after the Sino-Soviet Split, when Mao adopted an extremely activist, revolutionary foreign policy orientation (Yu 1977; Alden and Alves 2008; Brazinsky 2017; Cheng and Taylor 2017; Eisenman 2018). This expansion was significant: Even as hundreds of millions of Chinese citizens lived in poverty, Chinese government spending on foreign aid accounted for over 5 percent of the national budget by the early 1970s (Dreher et al. 2022). Chinese foreign aid was initially concentrated in nearby socialist states, but during the 1960s China began providing aid to dozens of countries in Asia, Africa, and other regions within the "Third World."

Revolutionary aid was fiscally unsustainable, and China experienced a role reversal and became a major net recipient of aid inflows during the reform and opening period. Its outgoing aid was scaled down and redirected toward smaller, economically sustainable projects under Deng Xiaoping. China concurrently began to receive high volumes of development finance, including many large-scale infrastructure projects, from donors and lenders like Japan and the World Bank. The Chinese government reengineered its development finance approach once again during the 1990s – a process discussed more in the following section – and returned to its status as a net provider of development finance around 2005 (Kobayashi 2008; Chin 2012).[9]

---

[9] Researchers often divide Chinese development finance into different periods based on these shifts. For example, Lin (1993) divides it into four periods: 1953–1963, 1964–1971, 1972–1978, and 1979–1989, whereas Kobayashi (2008) separates it into three: China as a net donor (1953–1978), net recipient (1978–1995), and emerging donor (post-1995). Dreher and Fuchs (2015) divide Chinese aid into five periods based on changing political and economic motives. Cheng and Taylor (2017) see China's aid to Africa as having four periods. Dreher et al. (2022) separate China's outward development finance into four periods largely reflective of China's domestic development situation.

These shifts are important for understanding the origins of China's contemporary global infrastructure drive. In particular, important policy changes during the early reform era helped position China to dramatically scale up its provision of overseas infrastructure. As China's economy incrementally opened up during the 1980s and 1990s, the Chinese government reoriented its outgoing development finance to chiefly serve commercial in addition to political purposes. This adjustment was informed by China's own experience hosting Japanese-financed infrastructure and other development projects. For example, Japan's government frequently utilized commodity-backed loans when financing infrastructure projects in China (Bräutigam 2009). It also adopted a project allocation approach in which China's government, often jointly with Japanese enterprises, directly proposed specific infrastructure projects for Japan to finance (Zhang and Smith 2017). Both of these features are now well-known attributes associated with many contemporary Chinese-financed infrastructure projects abroad.

Several specific policy changes also occurred during this period with consequences for Chinese global infrastructure. In 1982, China's Ministry of Commerce, at the time called the Ministry of Foreign Economic Relations and Trade (对外经济贸易部), established the Department of Foreign Aid (援助司) to manage overseas foreign assistance projects. Around the same time, China National Complete Plant Import & Export Corporation Ltd. (COMPLANT), which would eventually become a state-owned enterprise (SOE), was mandated with implementing most of China's overseas development projects. China's government also adopted a Contract Responsibility Mechanism (承包责任制) under which newly formed subsidiary enterprises of central and provincial government institutions, which would also eventually become SOEs, implemented Chinese-financed projects abroad (Cheng and Taylor 2017, 39–42). The government also began to encourage the creation of joint ventures between Chinese enterprises and foreign governments and firms, in part to support overseas development projects. Finally, the Chinese government started encouraging Chinese contractors to explore overseas markets as early as the 1970s, and Chinese construction companies began to accumulate experience as contractors for international infrastructure projects (Zhang 2020).

Commercialization of China's development finance accelerated further in the 1990s with the establishment of China's two primary "policy banks," the Export-Import Bank of China ("China Eximbank") and China Development Bank ("CDB"), which were created in part to take over underperforming domestic projects in China (Sanderson and Forsythe 2013). After their formation, Eximbank and CDB also began serving as the major financial vehicles through which China's government provided capital for infrastructure projects around the world, particularly through concessional loans. Collectively, these experiences, policy reforms, and new institutions provided the foundation for China's post-2000 global infrastructure drive.

The "Going Out" strategy launched by Jiang Zemin in the late 1990s and the BRI launched fifteen years later drove and accelerated China's global infrastructure spree. Both initiatives explicitly linked several national economic priorities with China's overseas development finance and mobilized immense state resources for financing and building infrastructure in developing countries. These objectives included finding alternative investment opportunities to US treasury securities and managing excess foreign exchange reserves; increasing foreign demand for Chinese goods and services, especially industrial inputs produced in excess; creating globally competitive, national champion firms; enhancing China's energy security; and attempting to wean China's own economy off of infrastructure investment (e.g. State Council 2013; Kong and Gallagher 2017; Ye 2020; Dreher et al. 2022). Relative to other development projects, infrastructure is particularly useful for pursuing many of these objectives as it offers massive financial and construction scale for allocating capital and supporting Chinese companies who serve as contractors.

The net result of these developments was that, by the early 2000s, China's government was no longer a "traditional" donor who provided most of its overseas development capital as concessional aid. Instead, it had transformed into a massive provider of infrastructure primarily financed by loans motivated just as much by commercial considerations as political goals (Dreher et al. 2022). China still remained an important aid donor during this transformation, and its provision of smaller, highly concessional foreign aid projects in agriculture, education, health, and various social sectors has also increased significantly since the 1980s and after 2000. But these projects now represent a shrinking share of China's overall global development footprint. China has taken on a hybrid role as a major source of both development aid and commercial infrastructure lending, though the latter is increasingly dominant as a share of China's overall development finance. For example, between 2000 and 2007 China committed 61 cents of aid for every dollar of lending committed (Dreher et al. 2022, 105). In contrast, from 2013 to 2017, it committed just 11 cents of aid for each dollar of lending (Malik et al. 2021).

This evolution has arguably made it more difficult for the Chinese government to consolidate its development finance program – an already strenuous task given a wide range of stakeholders – by further increasing the number of relevant political and commercial actors. The Ministry of Commerce (MOFCOM) has long been the primary actor in managing China's overseas development projects, but the Ministry of Foreign Affairs (MFA) as well as several domain-specific ministries, including the Ministry of Agriculture and Ministry of Health, have also long been involved with implementing Chinese-financed aid projects.

China's infrastructure-heavy development finance approach since 2000 significantly increased the pool of financial and policy stakeholders. These include, to name a few, sovereign funds that finance Chinese banks, China Eximbank and China Development Bank, China Export & Credit Insurance Corporation (Sinosure), other commercial banks involved with lending for Chinese-financed projects, Economic and Commercial Counselor Offices (ECCOs) (经济商务参赞处) attached to Chinese embassies abroad, and SOEs implementing projects on the ground in other countries. These actors play important roles across project financing and implementation (e.g. Gill and Reilly 2007; Corkin 2011).

Chinese SOEs serving as contractors and in other roles have become especially important infrastructure actors on the ground. They possess the expertise needed to build large-scale infrastructure projects in diverse foreign environments and, even as Chinese labor costs have increased, they can often do so at significantly lower costs than contractors from "traditional" donor and creditor countries (Huang and Chen 2016). State-owned enterprises are not passive actors who simply implement state directives, and available evidence shows that they can affect and interact with Chinese development finance in multiple ways. One study based on elite interviews with Chinese officials finds that Chinese SOEs and politicians in host countries can coordinate to secure infrastructure loans backed by Chinese policy banks, which impacts both the national and subnational allocation of projects (Zhang and Smith 2017).[10] Moreover, in recent years Chinese SOEs have expanded from their traditional roles as contractors responsible for engineering, procurement, and construction. They are increasingly playing more active roles in overseas infrastructure projects often involving more equity and risk. They are doing so through build-operate-transfer (BOT) and other forms of public-private partnerships, as well as emerging forms of stakeholder-ship such as "integrated investment, construction, and operation" (Leutert 2019; Zhang 2023).

Actor proliferation has likely made bureaucratic coordination more difficult. In 2018, China's government created the China International Development Cooperation Agency (CIDCA) to serve as an independent aid agency under the State Council and improve coordination (Rudyak 2019a). But CIDCA's vice-ministerial rank may circumscribe its relative authority, and thus far it

---

[10] This process is partially enabled by inadequate staffing across China's development finance bureaucracy (Zhang and Smith 2017).

remains unclear whether and the extent to which CIDCA or other new institutions can help streamline China's development finance bureaucracy. It remains to be seen whether these bureaucratic and commercial actors can coordinate effectively and minimize informational and operational inefficiencies, especially when implementing large, complex infrastructure projects (Zhao and Jing 2019). As discussed in Section 4, actor diversity also presents challenges for China's government in trying to leverage global infrastructure for its pursuit of international influence.

In summary, Chinese development finance has undergone multiple shifts over the past seven decades. China's shift from an aid donor to a hybrid, global provider of both aid and less concessional developmental capital reflects growing importance of economic motivations in addition to longstanding political motives. This evolution introduced a plethora of new state and commercial actors into China's development finance arena, and also paved the way for China's contemporary global infrastructure drive. As Section 3 demonstrates, however, overseas infrastructure has a long lineage that has survived diverse periods of Chinese development finance.

2.2 What Do We Know about Contemporary Chinese Global Development Projects?

China's reemergence as a major donor and lender since 2000 has sprouted a large literature focused on the nature and consequences of China's global development projects, including but not limited to infrastructure. This section summarizes evidence on the allocation and impacts of these projects.

2.2.1 Where Does China Finance Development Projects?

China's government publishes considerably less detailed information on its overseas development projects compared to other major donors and lenders. Without systematic official data, researchers initially struggled to accurately categorize and measure China's global development projects. Earlier studies tended to aggregate all of China's state-financed capital in developing countries into catch-all measures such as "aid."[11] But only a portion of China's international development projects resemble aid projects based on definitions set by multilateral bodies such as the Organisation for Economic Co-operation and Development's Development Assistance Committee (OECD-DAC) (Bräutigam 2011).

Differentiating between Chinese aid- and debt-financed projects is thus crucial. As Dreher et al. (2018) show, Chinese aid and debt have fundamentally

---

[11] See Strange et al. (2013) for a summary of these studies.

different features and motives, so it makes little sense to lump them together. In terms of aid (i.e. "official development assistance," or "ODA," as defined by the OECD-DAC), in recent years China's government has provided several billion dollars globally each year and would rank within the top ten bilateral donors worldwide. It thus has remained a major and important source of foreign aid. But China's debt-based development finance (i.e. "other official flows," or "OOF"), which is usually much less concessional than aid and primarily provided via China Eximbank and CDB loans closer to prevailing market rates, far outpaces lending from any other bilateral lender.

As China's development finance grew throughout the early 2000s, international observers primarily located in Western democratic countries became anxious. They worried that Beijing would be a "rogue donor" that deployed aid to strengthen corrupt dictators, extract natural resources, and undermine aid from "traditional" donors and creditors rather than help communities most in need of assistance (Naim 2007). Available evidence suggests that these accusations have largely not materialized (Dreher and Fuchs 2015). Instead, China's foreign aid is heavily concentrated in less developed, poorer countries with high levels of economic need (Dreher et al. 2022).

The Chinese government does employ aid to pursue strategic foreign policy objectives such as securing international diplomatic recognition and political support. Since the 1950s it has used aid as a carrot to cement its international diplomatic recognition and isolate Taiwan, a dynamic examined more in Section 4 (Kao 1988). For example, the prospect of economic assistance from China was an important factor in shaping Chad's decision to abandon (for the second time) diplomatic support for Taiwan in favor of the PRC in 2006 (Cheng and Shi 2009). A more recent example is the government of Nicaragua, who severed official ties with Taiwan in December 2021. Shortly after, the government inked several agreements for economic assistance from China, including a 12,000-unit social housing scheme as well as provisional agreements for other infrastructure including ports, railways, energy, and water projects.[12]

Employing aid for geopolitical interests makes China similar to, rather than different from, "traditional" donors and creditors in the OECD-DAC. For example, political economists have shown repeatedly that donor governments funnel more bilateral aid to governments serving on the United Nations Security Council (UNSC) to sway policy decisions there (e.g. Kuziemko and Werker 2006), and can also steer multilateral development finance to temporary UNSC

---

[12] www.globalconstructionreview.com/china-funds-major-social-housing-scheme-in-nicaragua/.

members or other strategically important recipient countries (e.g. Dreher, Sturm, and Vreeland 2009).

On the other hand, Chinese aid often differs from aid provided by other major donors and lenders in at least one important way. China's "no strings attached" approach often allows host country politicians to steer the selection, location, and branding of aid projects to a greater degree than projects financed by other large donors and lenders. As a result, Chinese aid can become a form of "unearned income" that host country leaders strategically manipulate and allocate to politically salient areas, especially during important political periods (Smith 2008). Dreher et al. (2019) find that Chinese-financed aid projects are heavily concentrated in the birth regions of African leaders, particularly in the lead-up to competitive elections. Unfortunately, this means that projects sometimes do not end up in places with strong socioeconomic need, as leader birth regions tend to be located in wealthier regions (Hodler and Raschky 2014). In contrast, neither debt-financed projects from China nor development projects financed by the World Bank exhibit this tendency. These null findings make sense: The World Bank is known for conducting extensive pre-project evaluations and screenings to guard against political capture, while China is not known for employing rigorous safeguards (Independent Evaluation Group 2010; Dornan and Brant 2014; Dreher et al. 2022).

Chinese debt financing follows a different allocative logic. The Chinese government's approach to financing overseas infrastructure and other capital follows an "encompassing accumulation" logic aimed at both commercial and political objectives (Lee 2017). Commercial calculations in particular have become increasingly important since 2000, and as mentioned earlier, several national economic objectives have driven Chinese development lending for the past two decades. Allocation of Chinese debt-financed projects reflects these priorities. Dreher et al. (2022) show that Chinese development projects financed with debt are most frequently located in large, stable economies that offer greater potential for large returns on investment and lower likelihood of default. Another recent study supports this intuition and suggests that Chinese-financed electrification projects increasingly are allocated to wealthier countries with lower investment risks and higher ex ante electrification rates (Sauer et al. 2022). However, debt-based finance – much of which supports large-scale infrastructure projects – also flows heavily into countries with higher levels of corruption and lower levels of democracy. This is perhaps because such an institutional environment – which often features less bureaucratic red tape, regulation, and public oversight – makes it easier for China's policy banks and companies to do business with their host country counterparts.

2.2.2 What Are the Impacts for Host Countries and Societies?

A related research agenda examines how Chinese-financed development projects affect the societies and economies in which they are implemented. On balance, Chinese development projects appear to create important economic benefits in the short run, but also introduce several different types of risks for host countries.

Despite skepticism by other major donors and creditors, China's global infrastructure push has been a welcome sight for many developing countries. Host countries throughout Asia, Africa, and beyond have enormous infrastructure gaps, and most bilateral and multilateral donors and creditors stopped financing infrastructure at scale decades ago. One estimate suggests that US$3.3 trillion in infrastructure investment is required globally through 2030, which equates to over US$350 billion more than current annual levels, in order to maintain current economic development forecasts (McKinsey Global Institute 2016).[13] Proponents of China's approach thus often point out that Beijing is financing urgently needed "hardware" otherwise unavailable to many developing countries (Moyo 2009; Lin and Wang 2017). Evidence suggests that Chinese infrastructure is indeed helping fill this massive gap. Chinese development projects – both those financed through aid and especially those financed with debt – improve socioeconomic development in the short term as projects are built and come online. Dreher et al. (2021) find robust evidence that Chinese projects increase economic growth and activity both nationally and locally. In the short run, they find that an additional development project boosts economic growth on average between .41 and 1.49 percentage points two years after project commitment. At the same time, there is little or no evidence that Chinese development projects undercut potential development gains produced by Western donors and lenders – another claim of the aforementioned "rogue donor" narrative.

Over longer periods of time, however, the net benefits of China's global infrastructure and other development projects are less clear. Short-term economic boosts created by Chinese projects occur alongside complex economic, political, environmental, social, and other challenges introduced by the same projects. Grasping the medium- and long-term net economic effects of development projects, including those financed and built by Chinese actors, is a much more difficult task.

The issue of debt sustainability offers an illustration of this complexity. On the one hand, scholars have repeatedly challenged the well-known but highly

---

[13] The global infrastructure gap is a major impetus for larger efforts to mobilize trillions of dollars to achieve the Sustainable Development Goals (Independent Group of Scientists 2019).

controversial "Debt Trap Diplomacy" narrative insinuating that China's government has been strategically luring borrower countries into its economic and political orbit by saddling them with unsustainable infrastructure debts (e.g. Bräutigam 2020; Bräutigam 2022). Careful analysis of several flagship BRI projects finds little evidence of debt trap motives.

On the other hand, debt-financed infrastructure by definition requires substantial borrowing by host country governments. One earlier study found that eight countries may face high risks of debt distress because of their planned pipelines of BRI infrastructure projects, and this was calculated before many developing countries' balance sheets significantly worsened following the outbreak of the COVID-19 pandemic (Hurley, Morris, and Portelance 2019). Another study suggests that debt challenges from Chinese-financed infrastructure are due to both scope – i.e. the sheer volume and scale of Chinese-financed infrastructure around the world – as well as the lack of transparency on the part of China's government and policy banks, and the requirements in some loan contracts for borrower countries to keep loan terms shielded from public view (Gelpern et al. 2022). A more recent analysis suggests that in recent years China's government has used US$240 billion – primarily in the form of People's Bank of China's (PBOC) currency swaps in Renminbi and additional loans – in bailing out debt-distressed host governments, many of whom initially pursued BRI infrastructure projects (Horn et al. 2023).

In addition to debt sustainability issues, measuring the net, long-term impacts of Chinese development projects on various socioeconomic outcomes is considerably more complicated than studying short-term indicators. It will nonetheless be an important task for researchers in the coming years as many BRI projects currently under implementation become operational.

China's overseas development projects produce a wide range of other consequences in addition to socioeconomic impacts. To name but a few, Chinese-financed aid and debt projects can help reduce conflict in African countries when they fill voids created from aid withdrawals by "traditional" providers of development finance (Strange et al. 2017). At the same time, debt-financed projects might instead fuel conflict by expanding the reach of the state or creating local grievances (Dreher et al. 2022). Large infrastructure projects in particular can also create negative environmental externalities. This has long been a source of concern for environmental advocates who worry that infrastructure projects can harm the natural environment – via air pollution, deforestation, water and sewage contamination, and other channels – if these risks are not internalized by project implementers. Many planned transportation corridors along the BRI fall on or near fragile ecosystems and important biodiversity areas across Southeast Asia, sub-Saharan Africa, and South America

(Hughes 2019; Yang et al. 2021). Commercially driven, debt-financed projects provided by China are not known to be subject to internal vetting processes that adequately internalize these environmental risks and put in place corresponding standards. One study finds that Chinese-financed projects accelerate deforestation but that this effect is most severe in countries with poor environmental regulations and law enforcement, while negative effects can be minimized in more stringent regulatory environments (BenYishay et al. 2016). Another study points out that energy projects financed by Chinese policy banks, particularly coal-fired power plants financed before President Xi Jinping's 2021 pledge to stop building them, use enormous amounts of water and raise important questions about water security and sustainability (Alkon et al. 2019).

2.3 New Evidence on China's Global Development Projects since 1949

Until about a decade ago, little systematic evidence existed for studying China's evolving overseas development portfolio. As noted earlier, the Chinese government is less forthcoming than other major donor and creditor governments in terms of providing detailed information on its overseas development activities. Several open-source research initiatives have recently emerged to help fill this informational gap. These efforts have made it possible for researchers to more holistically and objectively study China's global development finance using both quantitative and qualitative methods. Research organizations like AidData at William and Mary and a joint project between Boston University and Johns Hopkins University have produced and published large datasets on China's global development finance. In subsequent sections, this Element employs two recently published datasets to study China's provision of infrastructure projects since 1949.[14]

The first dataset is AidData's Chinese Official Finance Dataset, Version 2.0 (Custer et al. 2021; Dreher et al. 2022). This dataset was constructed and refined over the past twelve years in collaboration with an interdisciplinary team of scholars as well as hundreds of staff and students, primarily at William and Mary in the United States. The data are collected and refined using a publicly documented method called Tracking Underreported Financial Flows (TUFF) (Custer et al. 2023). Social scientists routinely use this database to analyze the aims and effects of China's overseas development projects on a variety of outcomes. The 2.0 version of the dataset includes over 13,000 project records of Chinese government commitments of overseas development finance between 2000 and 2017, and the recently-released 3.0 version extends data coverage through 2021.

---

[14] Data presented in this Element are subject to periodic update as underlying datasets are updated.

The second dataset is China's 20th-Century Global Development Projects, a new dataset I also developed along with a research team based at the University of Hong Kong. It includes all publicly known Chinese government-financed development projects worldwide committed between 1949 and 1999. Over the past three years, our research team developed and applied a data collection methodology that builds on the general principles of TUFF and makes particularly heavy use of historical Chinese government publications – including bilateral agreements, various other government documents, and Party-state-controlled newspapers – to track China's twentieth-century overseas development projects.

The dataset also benefits from and builds on earlier attempts to track twentieth-century Chinese global development activities (e.g. Horvath 1976; Law 1984; Bartke 1989; Lin 1993; Morgan and Zheng 2019).[15] Each of these efforts relied on a combination of official and unofficial sources to track Chinese-financed development projects in Africa and beyond. These earlier studies provide valuable evidence on China's evolving role in financing global development, but none of them produced a comprehensive accounting of Chinese development finance before 2000, whether in terms of the overall sample of projects or in terms of the specific details and sources for each project. The new dataset thus helps fill a longstanding gap in the literature.

The twentieth-century data also complement other recent initiatives that track contemporary China's overseas development finance – such as AidData as well as the Chinese Loans to Africa (CLA) Database – by enabling researchers to examine Chinese development projects since 1949 to the present day.[16] The historical dataset includes nearly 4,000 Chinese-financed development project commitments between 1949 and 1999 to over 130 countries.

Finally, these data are also valuable for studying Chinese global infrastructure projects, the focus of the remainder this Element. They help make three contributions in the proceeding sections. First, as mentioned in Section 1, the outpouring of policy and academic analysis on Chinese infrastructure suffers from recency bias and rarely offers historical context for the BRI. The historical data are compatible with contemporary datasets and, as shown in the following, enable analysis of Chinese overseas infrastructure projects over a long time horizon.

---

[15] Bartke (1989) used Chinese newspapers and other sources to construct a dataset of Chinese global development projects between 1956 and 1987. Both the OECD (1978) and Lin (1993) built on and extended this work, and the CIA (1982) also tracked various Chinese loans and grants provided to developing countries throughout the Cold War. More recently, Hawkins et al. (2010) produced project-level data on Chinese aid projects between 1990 and 2005 using MOFCOM yearbooks, and Morgan and Zheng (2019) used an approach adapted from TUFF to track pre-2000 projects in Africa.

[16] The dataset is compatible with data on contemporary Chinese-financed development projects gathered using AidData's TUFF methodology.

Second, in documenting China's twentieth-century development projects, our research team directly coded all of China's publicly known infrastructure projects. This is a departure from previous approaches that typically document Chinese development finance projects at the transaction- rather than project-level. The approach herein is novel because, despite a wide consensus that infrastructure is central to China's development cooperation, available datasets and research tend to measure and analyze infrastructure indirectly. As pointed out in Section 1, most quantitative research that makes use of public datasets employs proxies for infrastructure projects, such as dollars committed to infra-structure-intensive sectors or certain types of financing instruments, rather than analyzing actual infrastructure projects. In contrast, in building the dataset of historical Chinese development projects, we carefully coded every individual project for several infrastructure-related variables. Crucially, our research team also applied this infrastructure coding protocol to AidData's Chinese Official Finance Dataset, Version 2.0.[17] The data featured in the following section make use of this approach.

Third, and relatedly, measuring infrastructure requires a definition. Whereas earlier research often refers to Chinese overseas infrastructure in broad or vague terms, in the following section I first explicitly define different kinds of Chinese global infrastructure and then operationalize the definitions to catalog Chinese projects since 1949 using the aforementioned datasets.

3 Chinese Global Infrastructure: High-Profile and Prestige Projects

As discussed in the previous section, most existing research focuses on Chinese development finance generally rather than infrastructure specifically. This section first contextualizes popular debates on Chinese overseas infrastructure. It considers Chinese and general perspectives on infrastructure, then introduces a new definition – covering both "high-profile" and "prestige" projects – and applies it to empirically catalog China's global infrastructure since 1949.

3.1 Chinese and International Perspectives

China's overseas infrastructure is loosely defined concept without clear boundaries. Most analysts are plausibly referring to large, physical development projects with one or more tangible sites. Roads, railways, airports, harbors and ports, office buildings, housing complexes, power plants, factories, mines, industrial zones, government facilities, stadiums, and entertainment

---

[17] The 3.0 version includes a general binary marker for infrastructure, whereas I use a more specific measure of global infrastructure discussed below.

and meeting venues are among the most common types of Chinese infrastructure development projects. In addition, Chinese overseas infrastructure includes a growing portfolio of "digital infrastructure" such as wireless networks, artificial intelligence, smart cities and digital surveillance technologies, nanotechnology, and quantum computing projects (Xinhua 2017).

In conceptualizing Chinese global infrastructure, Chinese official and quasi-official interpretations are a natural starting point. The term "infrastructure" (基础设施), and related terms such as "infrastructure construction" (基础建设), began regularly appearing in Party-state-controlled newspapers in the 1980s. For example, across People's Daily (人民日报) articles published between 1950 and 2022, "infrastructure" appears regularly in the early 1980s and became a frequently mentioned topic thereafter. Much of the discussion, however, pertained to domestic infrastructure construction in China. Since then, as shown in Table 1, China's official conceptualization of infrastructure has gradually evolved over the past three decades. Infrastructure initially referred to physical projects seen as prerequisite foundations for economic development. Subsequent definitions continue to suggest that infrastructure is vital for socioeconomic development, and that it plays a "foundational, leading, and all-encompassing" (基础性、先导性、全局性) role. More recent interpretations highlight transportation and digital fields in particular, differentiating them as "traditional" and "new" infrastructure.

Chinese discussions of infrastructure built *outside of China* have often concentrated on three themes: the importance of "connectivity," the application of China's domestic infrastructure experience to the international realm, and, to a lesser extent, China's international influence. First, Chinese government speeches and documents, particularly those published since the launch of the BRI, emphasize the socioeconomic value of infrastructure connectivity. For instance, at the Belt and Road Forum in May 2017, Xi Jinping remarked:

> Infrastructure connectivity is the foundation of development through cooperation. We should promote land, maritime, air and cyberspace connectivity, concentrate our efforts on key passageways, cities and projects and connect networks of highways, railways and sea ports .... We need to seize opportunities presented by the new round of change in energy mix and the revolution in energy technologies to develop global energy interconnection and achieve green and low-carbon development. We should improve trans-regional logistics network and promote connectivity of policies, rules and standards so as to provide institutional safeguards for enhancing connectivity. (Xinhua 2017).

The Chinese government has continuously doubled down on this sentiment. At the third symposium on Belt and Road development in 2021, Xi emphasized

Table 1 Selected references to infrastructure in *People's Daily*, 1949–2022

Date	Infrastructure in Chinese text	Translation
11/09/1990	基础设施一般指能源、交通、邮电、江河流域治理、农田水利建设、环境保护以及供热、供水、供气等基本设施, 它是社会经济发展的基本物质条件。	Infrastructure generally refers to basic facilities such as energy, transportation, post and telecommunications, river basin management, agricultural irrigation and water conservancy, environmental protection, as well as heat, water and gas supply, which are the essential material conditions for social and economic development.
01/16/2017	基础设施互联互通是"一带一路"建设的优先领域 … 基础设施 (包括高速公路、大桥、高铁、港口、电厂、通讯设施等)。基础设施对经济社会发展具有基础性、先导性、全局性作用。	Infrastructure is a priority area of the "Belt and Road" initiative. Infrastructure (including highways, bridges, high-speed railways, ports, power plants, communication facilities, etc.). Infrastructure plays a fundamental, pioneering, and an all-encompassing role in economic and social development.
06/08/2020	传统基础设施建设主要指'铁公机', 包括铁路、公路、机场、港口、水利设施等建设项目, 在我国经济发展过程中具有重要的基础作用。新基建则主要指以 5 G、数据中心、人工智能、工业互联网、物联网为代表的新型基础设施, 本质上是信息数字化的基础设施。	Traditional infrastructure construction mainly refers to "RHA," including construction projects such as railways, highways, airports, ports, and water conservancy facilities, which have a fundamental role in China's economic development. New infrastructure construction,

Table 1 (cont.)

Date	Infrastructure in Chinese text	Translation
		on the other hand, mainly refers to 5G technology, data centers, AI, the industrial internet, and internet of things (IoT), which is essentially digitalized infrastructure.

that infrastructure is important for building "hard connectivity" (硬联通) along the BRI (Xi 2021).[18] The State Council's 2021 white paper on "International Development Cooperation in the New Era" also emphasized the role of infrastructure connectivity (State Council 2021). The National Development and Reform Commission (NDRC)'s Belt and Road Construction Promotion Center (国家发展改革委一带一路建设促进中心) added in January 2022 that infrastructure connectivity is a key priority of the BRI (People's Daily 2022). Chinese economists have argued that spatial connectivity created through overseas infrastructure generates economic value because it relieves bottlenecks such as unemployment and productivity, whereas Western bilateral and multilateral financiers' emphasis on social development lacks connectivity elements and has thus failed to provide these benefits (e.g. Lin and Wang 2017). In short, from the perspective of China's government and other observers, global infrastructure is a defining feature of Chinese international development cooperation, and one of its key functions is to promote "connectivity."

Another perspective is that overseas infrastructure projects are an outward reflection of China's own approach to promoting development at home. Both Chinese and international scholars have interpreted China's global infrastructure drive as the "internationalization of a development-finance model that has facilitated its own growth in the past decades" (Yeh and Wharton 2016; Chen 2020a, 437). This approach emphasizes economic "hardware" such as transportation infrastructure, for which China's government plays a central role in financing and projects and increasing their creditworthiness. Observers inside and outside of China point to large-scale infrastructure as China's clear comparative advantage over other donors and creditors that stems from its own development approach

---

[18] He also remarked that this connectivity should "deepen traditional infrastructure project cooperation and advance new forms of infrastructure project cooperation" (深化传统基础设施项目合作, 推进新型基础设施项目合作).

(Wang 2017; Wahba 2021). Over the past three decades, local, provincial, and national government actors invested hundreds of billions of dollars in upgrading China's transportation infrastructure. China's government began overhauling and expanding the highway system in the early 1990s, which spread out economic activity from large cities into surrounding areas and had potentially large, positive effects on average incomes (Roberts et al. 2012; Baum-Snow et al. 2017). Similarly, between 2004 and 2019, China built over 35,000 kilometers (km) of high-speed rail operating at a speed of at least 250 km/hour (Ma 2022, 2).[19] Beyond transportation projects, Chinese government agencies and state-owned enterprises at various administrative levels have also invested heavily in other large, physical infrastructures such as office buildings, malls, stadiums, performing arts centers, and event venues, to name but a few.[20]

A third perspective held by some within and outside of China parallels international debates discussed in Section 1: The potential for overseas infrastructure to enhance China's global influence. Even before the launch of the BRI, Chinese leaders purportedly believed that international infrastructure would increase China's global influence and advance its foreign policy interests. As Ye (2020, 177) points out, the idea of "infrastructure diplomacy" dates at least to 2008 when a blueprint for a "Chinese Marshall Plan" was laid out. Earlier generations of Chinese leaders also saw merit in deploying high-visibility infrastructure projects to pursue influence across Asia and Africa. One of China's most famous aid projects, the Tanzania–Zambia Railway (TAZARA, 坦赞铁路), was endorsed by Premier Zhou Enlai, who believed the project would generate substantially greater influence than would using the money to instead build small and medium-sized projects in other countries (Editorial Board 2008, 322; Monson 2021). Though TAZARA – and many other major Chinese infrastructure projects discussed in the following sections – was also heavily motivated by other economic and political objectives, the Chinese government perceived the project as an important conduit for pursuing international influence.

3.2 Infrastructure Promises and Pitfalls: Comparative Context

Beyond Chinese perspectives, earlier research and debates in other settings provides additional context for China's overseas infrastructure drive. For example, a large literature in economics suggests that government spending on infrastructure

---

[19] China's enormous domestic investments in high-speed rail and other transportation projects were subject to intense policy debate, and there is persistent uncertainty regarding their long-term profitability (e.g. Ma 2011; Ansar et al. 2016; Pettis 2022).

[20] The hosting of international events – also an impetus for host countries requesting Chinese infrastructure financing, as discussed below – often legitimized proposals for these projects in China (Ren 2017, 148).

generally has positive effects on economic productivity growth (e.g. Aschauer 1998; Sanchez-Robles 1998; Roller and Waverman 2001; Esfahani and Ramirez 2003). Infrastructure can generate short-run economic boosts by stimulating investment and employment, and can also produce long-term productivity increases as projects become active and begin to reshape economic activity (Leduc and Wilson 2013).[21] Big infrastructure projects in particular directly create new employment opportunities (e.g. Ali and Pernia 2003; Gibbons et al. 2019) which can be politically valuable to governments. On balance, existing research suggests infrastructure promotes economic growth, though there is less consensus over the precise channels and timing over which this occurs (Calderón and Servén 2014). International development actors have applied this economic rationale to prescribe infrastructure investment in developing countries, and international institutions such as the World Bank and International Monetary Fund (IMF) consistently emphasize the need for global infrastructure investment (e.g. World Bank 1994).

In terms of economic potential, at first glance China's global infrastructure push should thus be a welcome sight. Developing countries throughout the Global South have enormous infrastructure gaps, and Chinese-supported infrastructure promises to help address them. Available evidence, including that discussed in the previous section, generally supports the notion that Chinese-financed infrastructure stimulates economic activity in these countries. Dreher et al. (2022) find that Chinese debt-financed projects – including many big-ticket infrastructure projects – improve socioeconomic outcomes in the short run in host countries at national and local levels. These projects increase economic output, decrease child mortality, and reduce spatial inequality by alleviating bottlenecks. Transportation infrastructure projects in particular can lower the cost of commuting to and from cities and increase property values in suburban and rural communities in developing countries (Bluhm et al. 2021). Other recent studies report similar findings of positive, short-term economic impacts of Chinese infrastructure (e.g. De Soyres, Mulabdic, and Ruta 2020; Mueller 2022). There is also evidence that Chinese infrastructure projects abroad can increase local employment by stimulating short-term demand for low-skilled labor and longer-term demand for skilled labor after projects are finished, in countries such as Angola, Ethiopia, and Uganda (Warmerdam and van Dijk 2013; Guo and Jiang 2021; Oya and Schaefer 2023). Chinese-financed projects that mitigate infrastructure bottlenecks may also help local firms

---

[21] It can also affect inequality directly and indirectly by providing new economic opportunities and increasing the value of assets owned by less wealthy members of the population. Transportation infrastructure can increase the productivity of transport-reliant sectors, lower commute costs, and unlock economic opportunities for communities and households (Fernald 1999; Donaldson 2018).

become more productive, particularly those lacking access to quality transportation options (Marchesi, Masi, and Paul 2021).

Over the longer term, evidence from other contexts is less conclusive about whether large infrastructure drives sustainable growth in developing countries (e.g. Warner, Berg, and Pattillo 2014). Assessing the economic impacts of large infrastructure projects is difficult because of their scale, long implementation time, and financial and operational complexity (Leduc and Wilson 2013). On the one hand, these projects usually possess outsized economic ambitions that are not captured by short-term changes. Big infrastructure is not merely about direct, short-term results, and often hinges on grander visions of reshaping socioeconomic activity within or across communities of various scales. For example, city and other administrative governments in the United States undertook large public infrastructure projects at an unprecedented scale in the 1950s and 1960s, as a strategy aimed at revitalizing urban centers by attracting private and commercial investment (Altshuler and Luberoff 2003).

While transformational ambitions make large-scale infrastructure appealing, they also inject major economic risks for project and community stakeholders. Even if infrastructure projects increase aggregate welfare, they also often create highly uneven distributional consequences (e.g. Duflo and Pande 2007). Other studies question the basic economic viability of large infrastructure. Scholars of "megaprojects," often defined as multibillion dollar transformational projects, have studied this phenomenon extensively. In their global study, Flyvbjerg et al. (2003; 2017, 12) suggest that these projects follow "iron laws": the majority are consistently "over budget, over time, under benefits, over and over again." Drawing on evidence from several hundred projects, they find that megaprojects are highly prone to economic underperformance across different political and geographic environments. Another study examines over 300 industrial megaprojects and similarly finds that over 65 percent "failed to meet business objectives" (Merrow 2011, vii). "Megastructures," or "massive construction or structure[s], especially a complex of many buildings," have also historically yielded subpar economic and publicity results given their enormous scale, cost, and lengthy time horizons (Banham 2020, 16). These tendencies are no less likely in developing countries, where infrastructure has always tended to take longer than expected to implement (Calderón and Servén 2014; Estache and Fay 2007).[22]

---

[22] Many other projects are simply never finished. For instance, one study examines over 14,000 small infrastructure projects in Ghana and finds that one-third are never completed (Williams 2017).

Other researchers have similarly documented how government investments in infrastructure and other large-scale interventions often disappoint. Scott (1998, 5) shows how high-modernist ideologies that became prevalent during the second half of the eighteenth century convinced governments to attempt to reorder societies around infrastructural interventions such as "huge dams, centralized communication and transportation hubs, large factories and farms, and grid cities." Developing countries, many of which were still colonies at the time, were often experimental sites for these interventions as colonial governments sponsored infrastructure projects that envisioned socioeconomic transformation and justified repression (Lorenzini 2019, 13–14).

When governments become captivated by infrastructure visions and promises, they also can struggle to identify and select socially optimal projects. As Anand, Gupta, and Appel (2018, 19) explain, "Shiny new airports with huge capacities are built in many countries although they only serve a tiny elite, whereas less glamorous infrastructures, which would actually be more useful to the poorer segments of the population, are ignored and overlooked." Alternatively, even if governments are relatively clear-eyed regarding infrastructure investment costs and benefits, political incentives can lead them to investment large sums in socioeconomically wasteful infrastructure (e.g. Robinson and Torvik 2005).

Several other factors can further help explain large-scale infrastructure's fraught economic performance. Proponents of major infrastructure are prone to tendencies and biases that can jeopardize objective calculation. Political leaders may desire the "rapture" from "building monuments to themselves" and from the "visibility this generates with the public and media," while project architects, planners, and consumers may derive "pleasure" from "building and using something very large that is also iconic and beautiful" (Flyvbjerg 2017, 6). These and other individual-level "sublimes" can lead project supporters to neglect thorough cost-benefit analyses and subvert potential opposition voices that would otherwise serve as accountability mechanisms. Flyvbjerg et al. (2003, 5) note that even in democratic contexts, project advocates often shun "established practices of good governance, transparency and participation in political and administrative decision making." The sheer financial and operational scale and complexity of large infrastructure further make it vulnerable to a suite of challenges, including corruption, public-private coordination bottlenecks, lack of flexibility, and bias toward linear thinking.

Existing research suggests that China's overseas infrastructure projects display many of these basic features. Chinese government-financed projects are similarly large, complex, and have long time horizons that complicate cost-benefit analysis. For example, Kaplan (2021) describes Chinese overseas development loans for infrastructure as "patient capital" with long time horizons, high risk tolerance, and low conditionality relative to capital from other foreign creditors. Other scholars have similarly noted that "the costs and benefits of large-scale infrastructure construction cannot be conclusively determined through a set of standard meas-urements; rather, many contributing factors must be observed and analyzed over the long term" (Tang 2021, 81–82).

These general pitfalls of large infrastructure should also sound familiar to observers of the BRI. For example, Chinese government-financed infrastruc-ture and other development projects may insulate host governments from potential opposition. One study finds that natural resource-related project financing from China reduces "horizontal" legislative and judicial account-ability, but has no effect on "vertical" accountability between rulers and their constituents (Ping, Wang, and Chang 2022). Development projects provided by the Chinese government are also associated with higher levels of corrup-tion in local communities that host them (Brazys, Elkink, and Kelly 2017; Isaksson and Kotsadam 2018). In particular, large-scale infrastructure – which tends to be located in relatively corrupt and undemocratic countries – may further exacerbate accountability and governance issues in already corrupt business environments. Infrastructure projects can do so by creating new interest groups or strengthening and augmenting existing ones composed of political and business elites (e.g. Camba 2021).[23]

The tendency for large infrastructure to encounter delays is also frequently cited along the BRI. One study examines 431 Chinese-financed development projects and finds that more than half were completed behind schedule (Malik et al. 2021, 132). The same study finds that ninety-one projects that underper-formed compared to their initially stated objectives in terms of profits, debt repayments, or implementation milestones. As an example, the Chinese-financed high-speed railway in Laos experienced major delays in allocating credit for different phases of the project. This has slowed overall progress and also left various intended beneficiaries – including Chinese SOEs as well as Chinese and Laotian workers – worse off (Chen 2020b). On the other hand, roughly a quarter of projects for which there is information on both start and end dates were reportedly completed *ahead* of schedule. Kenya's SGR is one well-known example of infrastructure along the BRI completed ahead of time (Wang 2022).

In short, Chinese overseas infrastructure projects exhibit many of the proper-ties and tendencies associated with infrastructure in other contexts. It is also

---

[23] On the other hand, Chinese aid and debt does not necessarily work in the way that the "rogue donor" narrative would suggest. Bader (2015), for instance, finds no evidence that Chinese aid improves the prospects of political survival for autocrats abroad.

possible that big-ticket infrastructure loans provided by Chinese policy banks may produce even greater vulnerability to economic miscalculation on the part of China's government, borrower governments, contractor firms, or other stakeholders due to opaque lending practices. On the other hand, however, being able to point to examples of efficient implementation is likely an important priority for China's government given that speed and efficiency, especially relative to "traditional" donors and lenders, has become one of its reputational cornerstones. In any case, assessing the net socioeconomic impacts of overseas Chinese infrastructure projects, and infrastructure projects in general, is an arduous task given these projects' scale, complexity, long time horizons, and multidimensional impacts.

3.3 Conceptualizing Chinese Global Infrastructure

Researchers in other fields have provided a variety of definitions for infrastructure, but none are ideally suited for studying Chinese infrastructure in the Global South. For example, infrastructure can refer broadly to "vast, complex, and changing systems that support modern societies and economies" (Carse 2016), or "the physical components of interrelated systems providing commodities and services essential to enable, sustain, or enhance societal living conditions" (American Society of Civil Engineers 2017). Other researchers have studied related concepts that overlap with infrastructure. "Megaprojects" are defined as "large-scale, complex ventures that typically cost $1 billion or more, take many years to develop and build, involve multiple public and private stakeholders, are transformational, and impact millions of people" (Flyvbjerg 2017, 2). Anthropologists have argued that infrastructure possesses important cultural, social, and political dimensions in addition to financial and economic concerns, highlighting both its material and immaterial functions. Larkin (2013, 328) defines it as "built networks that facilitate the flow of goods, people, or ideas and allow for their exchange over space" that are both dependent on and constitutive of local context. Anand, Gupta, and Appel (2018, 3) further note that "material infrastructures, including roads and water pipes, electricity lines and ports, oil pipelines and sewage systems, are dense social, material, aesthetic, and political formations that are critical both to differentiated experiences of everyday life and to expectations of the future."[24]

---

[24] Others point out that infrastructure is both relational and ecological and means different things to different groups (Star 1999). Local communities and individuals who interact with infrastructure forge group identities around it (Fredericks 2018). Another related term is "modernization," or a country's attempt "to upgrade its infrastructure to achieve a status that would put it on equal terms with the great powers" (Denicke 2011, 185).

These definitions are helpful starting points for Chinese global infrastructure. However, the concepts of "infrastructure" and "megaprojects" are broad and encompass many projects and initiatives beyond the realm of international development. These general definitions can also lead to problematic measurement. For example, in the context of Chinese development finance, "infrastructure" would capture thousands of small-scale, local projects unlikely to be consequential for Chinese influence or other national- or international-level outcomes. Similarly, the US$1 billion threshold for a megaproject does not account for country context and has limited use for development finance projects since host countries have differently sized economies; one billion dollars means different things in different places. If applied to Chinese development finance, "megaprojects" would include many financially large projects that are nonetheless relatively inconsequential for studying influence or other outcomes of interest. Conversely, looking only at projects valued over US$1 billion would omit hundreds of infrastructure projects with potentially important influence or other consequences.

Consider a recent Chinese-financed infrastructure project as an example. In 2016, the Chinese government committed a US$80 million grant for the 15 MW Ruzibazi Hydroelectric Power Plant in Burundi. The plant represents over 2 percent of Burundi's GDP and is one of the largest hydropower projects in the country. In contrast, it would rank outside the top 20 power generation projects that China's government has financed in Indonesia over the same period.

I define Chinese global infrastructure as high-visibility, national-level physical infrastructure projects financed by China's government in other countries.[25] Given the immense diversity of Chinese state, quasi-state, and non-state actors involved in overseas development activities, this definition is not meant to capture every single aspect of Chinese overseas infrastructure. For example, it omits projects financed by non-Chinese entities and built by Chinese contractors, even though this is also an already large and growing component of China's global development footprint (e.g. Leutert 2019; Zhang 2020). Nor does this definition include projects financed by China's government but not carried out by Chinese companies or other actors. It also omits small-scale, auxiliary, low-visibility, or other infrastructure unlikely to constitute highly visible, national projects.[26]

---

[25] This includes all infrastructure projects financed by any part of China's government, including Chinese policy and other state-owned and state-controlled banks.

[26] Examples of these include boreholes and wells; electrification schemes, transmission, and powerlines; telecommunications and surveillance technologies; satellites; and small-scale transportation, energy, and industrial projects.

Instead, this definition is designed to measure Chinese-financed and -built infrastructure projects that are global in character relative to other types of international development projects. Global infrastructure projects are negotiated bilaterally between governments, but these projects engage both state and non-state actors and produce local, national, and even global socioeconomic, political, environmental, and other consequences. They are also more likely to be salient in local, national, and global debates involving a wide range of actors. For these reasons, global infrastructure is also more likely than other Chinese development projects to produce influence or other political consequences for both host country governments and the Chinese government (the focus of Section 4).

Chinese global infrastructure spans an extremely diverse set of projects that generally share two important traits. First, relative to other forms of development finance, global infrastructure projects are highly visible. They have an outsized physical presence and also generate higher levels of publicity locally, nationally, and globally. Physical visibility correlates with project size and involves tangible and large or centrally located project sites. Media presence involves heavy publicity, particularly around project milestones such as announcement, groundbreaking, and completion ceremonies featuring rituals and performances, ribbon-cuttings, speeches by leaders, or other conspicuous activities (e.g. Menga 2015, 485). As discussed in the next section, visibility is an important feature that enables host country governments to brand infrastructure projects and advertise them to large audiences at home and abroad (e.g. Hirschman 1967; Dietrich, Mahmud, and Winters 2018; Baldwin and Winters 2020). Second, and relatedly, global infrastructure is national in scope within host countries. Financially and spatially large infrastructure, typically negotiated by (or at least involving approval from) national governments and possessing high visibility, is more likely to be salient in national political discourse within host countries compared to other projects.

China's government has primarily financed two types of global infrastructure since 1949, which are outlined in Table 2.[27] First, high-profile infrastructure projects are massive economic projects typically motivated by a mix of commercial and political considerations (Strange 2023a). High-profile infrastructure has comprised the bulk of Chinese global infrastructure and encompasses flagship, big-ticket infrastructure projects that have come to symbolize the BRI. As the next section illustrates, this project class mostly includes transportation, energy, and other economic infrastructure.

---

[27] These categories are of course not exhaustive and represent a first step. For example, socially oriented infrastructure projects such as national-level schools, hospitals, and agricultural infrastructure are not included in the below analysis, but could be incorporated in future research.

Table 2 Comparing high-profile and prestige infrastructure project features

	High-profile	**Prestige**
Visibility	High	High
Host country scope	National-level	National-level
No. projects, pre-2000	>300	>120
No. projects, post-2000	>900	>250
Avg. size, post-2000	~US$ 371 million	~US$ 29 million
Host countries	Global South	Small states in the Global South
Complexity	High	Low to medium
Commercial motive	Strong	Weak
Concessional	Sometimes	Usually
Host country symbolism	Sometimes	Usually
Common examples	Infrastructure projects in transportation, industry, energy, and other economic sectors (see Figure 2)	Government buildings; conference and convention venues; sports facilities; performing arts venues (see Figure 3)

In addition to being highly visible and nationally salient, high-profile infrastructure generally possesses two additional, related features that make it a distinct form of political capital for both host governments and China's government. First, relative to other development projects, high-profile infrastructure is financially and operationally large. Since 2000, the typical high-profile project has cost several hundred million dollars, and many of these projects have cost more than US$1 billion. In contrast, the average Chinese foreign aid project commitment since 2000 has cost less than 10 percent of a high-profile project, or approximately US$23.7 million. High-profile infrastructure is also physically sizable, encompassing one or more large project sites. Sheer scale makes high-profile infrastructure inherently different than smaller, locally focused projects. High-profile infrastructure is often envisioned by its planners as being "trait making" rather than "trait taking," with the potential to transform rather than simply fit into existing local economic and social structures (Hirschman 1967, vii, xi). As such, high-profile infrastructure is not merely about direct economic impact and often involves longer-term visions of reshaping socioeconomic activity at scale.

Second and relatedly, high-profile infrastructure is complex in terms of its configuration of stakeholders, financial structure, and operations. High-profile projects often involve constellations of domestic and foreign actors – such as central governments of the host and financing countries, local and regional governments, multilateral development institutions, foreign and local firms, and foreign and local workers – who perform different project functions such as financing, design, implementation, operations, and monitoring (Winters 2019; Strange, Plantan, and Leutert 2023). These projects also involve longer implementation timelines, more detailed and lengthier contracts, and relatively complicated financing arrangements.

Prestige projects are the second class of Chinese global infrastructure discussed in this Element. Like high-profile projects, prestige infrastructure is a well-known component of Chinese development finance. According to earlier accounts, Chinese overseas prestige projects include national-level government buildings, stadiums and other large sports facilities, convention and exhibition centers, and performing arts and cultural venues that are national in scope (Tull 2006; Bräutigam 2011; Swedlund 2017).

Most prestige projects have been financed as nonrepayable turnkey or "complete projects" (成套项目) in which China's government is responsible for project design, construction, and maintenance.[28] Chinese financing for prestige infrastructure is typically provided via nonrepayable grants or interest-free or otherwise highly concessional loans. A relatively small group of politically connected Chinese design and construction companies can bid for contracts from China's MOFCOM and profit from implementing prestige projects abroad. However, these projects, which are on average much financially smaller compared to high-profile projects, are driven primarily by host country demands and Chinese political interests outlined in Section 4.

These projects are much less expensive than high-profile infrastructure but can still have an outsized presence in some host countries. One reason for this is that prestige projects can serve as national symbolic capital for host country governments.[29] Political symbols are difficult to define due to their ubiquity (e.g. Edelman 1972; Dittmer 1977; O'Neill 2001), and national symbols here refer generally to representations of national themes or ideas embedded in

---

[28] By the early 1970s China had already financed and built approximately 100 turnkey projects (Bräutigam 2011, 41).

[29] High-profile infrastructure can also be nationally symbolic, but this is not necessarily a defining or prerequisite feature.

infrastructure projects. Prestige projects themselves can become national symbols or instead can transmit higher-level, national ideals such as modernity, progress, or unity (Steinberg 1987; van der Westhuizen 2007). As discussed in Section 4, host governments in the Global South typically frame prestige projects around themes of national identity, development, progress, and modernity, and also situate them in the context of a country's regional or international status ambitions.

3.4 Measuring Chinese Global Infrastructure

This section measures Chinese global infrastructure projects by operationalizing the definitions introduced in Section 3.3. I carefully combed over each development project that China's government has financed during the twentieth and twenty-first centuries using the aforementioned datasets, and identified physical infrastructure projects financed by China's government since 1949. These were then classified as high-profile, prestige, or other (non-global) types of infrastructure (Strange 2023a; Strange 2023b).

This approach provides a more direct, sharper measure of Chinese global infrastructure than earlier research. As an example, consider the transportation sector, an infrastructure-heavy sector often used to proxy for infrastructure. The two datasets collectively include over 1,200 project records in the Transport and Storage sector within the OECD's Creditor Reporting System (CRS). Individually coding infrastructure projects demonstrates that this sector contains over 700 actual unique infrastructure projects. About 450 of these fit the definition of either high-profile or prestige projects. Nearly half of the project records included in the transport sector are in fact additional financial transactions; surveying, maintenance, or other supplementary work; supplementary or auxiliary sub-infrastructures for a larger project; follow-on phases for an existing project; Chinese bank contributions to syndicated loans for projects not primarily financed or built by Chinese actors; or otherwise vague projects without sufficient information about a specific project.[30] Directly coding unique infrastructure projects provides a more accurate picture of when and where the Chinese government has supported global infrastructure across the Global South.

Using these definitions reveals that China's government has financed over 1,500 unique global infrastructure projects since 1949.[31] The Chinese government

---

[30] Unlike earlier studies, I exclude "maintenance" project records that represent follow-up activities to ongoing projects. This primarily includes feasibility studies, additional financing for an earlier project, maintenance work on physical project sites, dispatching of experts, or technical assistance to existing projects. I include expansion, renovation, revitalization, and modernization projects that involve significant new project activity.

[31] This figure is considerably higher if maintenance projects for existing Chinese-financed infrastructure are included, though I exclude these projects in this Element.

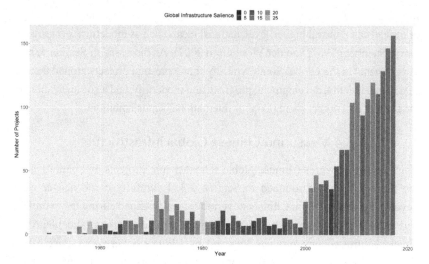

Figure 1 Global Infrastructure salience in Chinese overseas development
projects, 1949–2017

*Source: Custer et al. (2021); Dreher et al. (2022); Strange (2023a). More lightly shaded
bars indicate a higher level of salience, which is measured as the percentage of all Chinese
development projects that are global infrastructure projects committed in a given year.*

committed over 400 Chinese global infrastructure during the twentieth century.
The data also contain over 5,000 physical infrastructure projects, including both
global as well as other smaller and less visible infrastructure projects, approximately 1,500 of which were provided before 2000.

Combining data on China's twentieth- and twenty-first-century global infrastructure provides useful context for the BRI. Figure 1 plots the number of global
infrastructure projects – including both high-profile and prestige projects – committed annually by China's government since 1949.[32] It illustrates, in line with
previous research, that the sheer annual volume of Chinese global infrastructure
rose dramatically after the "Going Out" strategy and again after the launch of the
BRI. However, it also shows that global infrastructure was actually equally or
more salient as a share of China's total development projects during the first two
decades of the PRC. Global infrastructure was a major project class well before
China's development finance was reoriented to support national economic objectives outlined in the "Going Out" strategy and reinforced under the BRI. Over
a quarter of all of China's global infrastructure across the Global South to date
was committed before 2000.

---

[32] Figure B1 in the online Appendix plots the annual salience of high-profile and prestige
infrastructure separately and shows similar trends.

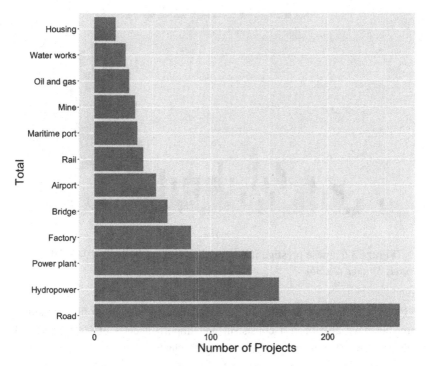

Figure 2 Most common Chinese high-profile infrastructure project types, 1949–2017

Note: These totals are approximations based on keyword searches of high-profile project titles and descriptions.

Source: Strange (2023a).

High-profile projects have accounted for the majority of Chinese global infrastructure. The data include nearly 1,200 high-profile projects in over 120 countries since 1949. Figure 2 plots the most common types of high-profile projects that China's government has financed and built in developing countries since 1949. The pre- and post-2000 distributions are similar and show that transportation infrastructure such as roads, bridges, airports, railways, and maritime ports collectively account for over a third of China's high-profile projects. Power generation infrastructure has been the other major project type and represents approximately a quarter of all high-profile projects. Figure B2 (online Appendix) maps the global distribution of high-profile infrastructure and Table A1 (online Appendix) lists the top host countries in terms of the number of projects. These major infrastructure projects have historically been most heavily concentrated in throughout various regions of Africa and Asia. High-profile infrastructure has been particularly prolific in Southeast Asia, and Cambodia, Indonesia, Myanmar, and Vietnam are all among the top host countries.

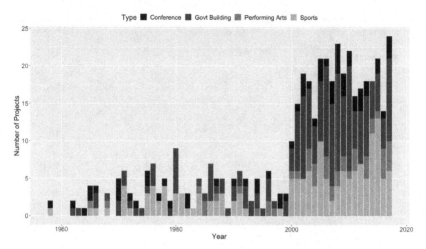

Figure 3 Chinese prestige infrastructure projects by type, 1949–2017
Source: Strange (2023b).

Prestige projects are smaller and less numerous than high-profile infrastructure, but have also been a consistent and important class of Chinese global infrastructure. They have appeared in roughly ninety developing countries since 1949, and as Figure 3 (and Table A2 in the online Appendix) show, China's government has financed and constructed nearly 400 prestige projects since 1950. Over 120 of these were financed before 2000. In both the twentieth and twenty-first centuries, China has financed hundreds of prestige projects in the form of government buildings, stadiums, conference venues, and entertainment and cultural venues.[33] Figure B3 in the online Appendix maps the global allocation of prestige projects since 1949. It illustrates that China's government has allocated prestige projects mostly in developing countries located in Asia, Africa, and in small island regions such as Oceania and the Caribbean. Among African countries, DRC, Sierra Leone, Tanzania, and Guinea are all among the top host countries. Small island states such as Samoa, Cape Verde, Comoros, Vanuatu, and Antigua and Barbuda are also among the most common host states.

High-profile and prestige infrastructure both constitute high-visibility, nationally salient projects, but China's government has different motivations for financing them abroad. High-profile projects are typically heavily or at least partially motivated by commercial and development objectives. Their visibility and national presence – combined with their sheer material and financial scale, operational and financial complexity, and long time horizons – makes them textbook risky infrastructure projects as outlined in Section 2. In other research,

---

[33] This is a conservative estimate that focuses only on these well-known project types.

I examine the factors that shape the global allocation of high-profile infrastructure and find that commercial considerations play an important role (Strange 2023a). This finding is largely consistent with that of Dreher et al. (2022), who show that debt-financed projects from China follow a commercial logic.

In contrast, prestige infrastructure is smaller and less heavily motivated by economic considerations on the part of host country governments, China's government, and other state or non-state actors on either side. In my research on prestige infrastructure, I instead find that these projects are heavily concentrated in the smallest states in the Global South whose leaders can request, acquire, and strategically brand Chinese-financed prestige projects as symbolic national achievements. My analysis shows that prestige project allocation is also associated with lower levels of economic development and smaller populations (Strange 2023b). In contrast, prestige projects have not been more likely to flow to more or less democratic governments. This suggests that these projects are not merely driven by host country leaders operating in highly clientelistic or institutionally weak political environments who need to rely on private goods provision to stay in office (e.g. Bueno de Mesquita et al. 2003; Robinson and Torvik 2005).

Global infrastructure's historical lineage is notable given important shifts in China's approach to overseas development finance outlined in Section 2. While its global infrastructure initially peaked in the 1970s at the height of Mao's revolutionary foreign policy, China continued to finance and build these projects albeit at a more modest scale during the 1980s and 1990s. Consider Chinese-financed prestige projects. By the middle of the 1980s, China's government was squarely in the early reform and opening period and intent on recalibrating and downsizing its overstretched aid campaign. Nonetheless, in 1980 China and Cape Verde signed an Economic and Technical Cooperation Agreement (经济技术合作协议)–a framework agreement commonly used throughout the twentieth century for China's overseas development project agreements–wherein China agreed to fund the construction of a parliamentary hall in Cape Verde. The project was previously suspended, but in July the two sides finalized an agreement for a US$13.2 million loan. Construction began less than two years later and the 12,000-square meter building was finished in 1985. The same year, China financed and built a People's Palace in Sao Tome and Principe. Other types of prestige projects, such as sports stadiums, also remained as stable fixtures in China's overseas financing portfolio, as shown by Figure 3. In October 1985, Senegalese President Abdou Diouf attended the completion ceremony of a China-aided Football Stadium in Dakar financed with a US$12 million loan initially conceived in 1973 and implemented by China National Corporation for Overseas Economic

Cooperation (CCOEC, 中国海外经济合作总公司). The stadium broke ground in 1982, and upon completion had a capacity of 60,000 spectators.

The aggregate statistics mentioned above illustrate the long pedigree of Chinese global infrastructure, but they do not capture the outsized stature of many important individual projects. Global infrastructures continue to occupy a central role in China's overseas development program and include many of its most famous (and infamous) projects. The aforementioned TAZARA Railway is perhaps the most fabled and well-studied example (See Figure 4). National leaders from Tanzania, Zambia, and China all played a crucial role in realizing the project (Brazinsky 2017, 297). In the summer of 1965, Zhou Enlai submitted an offer to Tanzanian President Nyerere to construct the railway, which the World Bank had refused to fund under pressure from the US and UK (Ismael 1971; Monson 2009). In September 1967, China's government agreed to finance and construct the railway with an interest-free loan valued at CNY988 million repayable over 25 years after a five-year grace period. One of the rationales for TAZARA would be to provide a transport route for Zambian exports to the Tanzanian coast. The railway was completed in June 1975 after five years of construction and follow-up agreements. During peak project implementation, it involved an estimated 38,000 Tanzanian and Zambian workers and 13,500 Chinese technical and engineering personnel. The line runs for 1860 km from Dar es Salaam in Tanzania to Kapiri Mposhi in Zambia. In addition to the original railway financing and construction, the historical dataset discussed earlier includes dozens of follow-up project activities on TAZARA

Figure 4 TAZARA railway (坦赞铁路)

Source: CIDCA.

including additional loans and grants, equipment donations, technical assistance and cooperation, and maintenance on TAZARA, which remains in operation today. The railway reportedly handled under 10 percent of cargo brought into Tanzania from the Port Dar es Salaam as of 2022, and China's government is planning to help revive it once again.[34]

TAZARA is one of hundreds of high-profile infrastructure projects China funded and built in the Global South during the twentieth century. Several years earlier, it agreed to provide an interest-free loan to build a hydroelectric dam and power station at Guinea's Kinkon Falls (金康水电站), which, like TAZARA, had failed to secure Western financing after Guinea's former colonial ruler, the French government, judged that the project was not viable (Zhou and Xiong 2017). Construction began in July 1964 about 400 km from the capital of Conakry. When completed, Guinea's deputy foreign minister attended the inauguration and handover ceremony of the 235-meter-long, 4x800KW dam. Today, the hydropower station appears on the Guinean franc (5,000 Francs Guinéens). The 20,000 franc banknote features the Kaleta Dam, another Chinese-financed high-profile infrastructure project that was constructed approximately 200 km west of Kinkon Falls nearly five decades later (Searsey 2015).

Prestige projects also became common shortly after China's government started providing overseas development finance. In February 1964, Zhou Enlai visited Ceylon (Sri Lanka) and received a request from President Sirimavo Bandaranaike to assist with the construction of an international conference center. The Chinese government agreed and the project, the Bandaranaike Memorial International Conference Hall (纪念班达拉奈克国际会议大厦), broke ground in late 1970 after a multiyear delay caused by opposition from the incumbent Third Dudley Senanayake cabinet. Shown in Figure 5, it was completed in 1973 and is still in operation today following several renovations and upgrades.

These projects, in addition to any economic goals, were also intended to advance China's policy goals and win popular approval – dynamics explored in Section 4 – during a time when China's overseas aid was unabashedly politically motivated. But Chinese global infrastructure projects also appeared during periods when China's development finance was less politicized and more economically oriented, such as the early reform and opening period.[35] In 1977, as China's revolutionary foreign policy began to subside, the governments of China and Mauritania inked a protocol to build Mauritania's Nouakchott Friendship Port (努瓦克肖特友谊港). China's government used a long-term, interest-free loan estimated to be worth over

---

[34] www.scmp.com/news/china/diplomacy/article/3189645/50-years-chinese-role-africas-freedom-railway-zambia-tanzania.

[35] Some infrastructure projects were formally committed or under implementation at the time of a Chinese policy shift and were still eventually completed.

Figure 5 Bandaranaike memorial international conference hall (纪念班达拉奈
克国际会议大厦)

*Source: Country (Region) Guide for Foreign Investment and Cooperation: Sri Lanka
2021(对外投资合作国别 (地区) 指南 斯里兰卡 2021年版), Embassy of the People's
Republic of China in Sri Lanka ECCO and Chinese Academy of International Trade and
Economic Cooperation (CAITEC).*

US$150 million. The port was completed and handed over to Mauritania's govern-
ment in July 1986, making it Mauritania's first deep-water port and China's second-
largest aid project after TAZARA (Shi 1989, 145, 199, 202–203). Other forms of
Chinese-financed transportation infrastructure continued to proliferate throughout
the 1970s and 1980s. After it severed diplomatic ties with Taiwan in 1972,
Madagascar signed an Economic and Technical Cooperation Agreement in
July 1975 in which China agreed to assist with the construction of the Moramanga-
Andranonampango   Highway   (木腊芒加至昂德拉努南邦古公路).   Phase
I construction began in December 1978 and the 83.6-km highway was completed
by the end of 1985, as displayed in Figure 6. Madagascar's president attended the
completion ceremony for the road, which was funded with an interest-free loan from
the Chinese government.

China's government continued to finance and build prestige and, to a lesser
extent, high-profile infrastructure during the 1980s and 1990s even as it became
a net aid recipient and focused on smaller, economically pragmatic overseas
projects. In January 1979 it began construction on the Palais des Congrés de Kara
(卡拉会议大厦) in Togo, which was finished in 1982, shortly after the completion
of another prestige project, Togo's Palais des Congrès de Lomé. High-level officials

Figure 6 Moramanga-Andranonampango highway (木腊芒加至昂德拉努南邦古公路)

Source: COMPLANT.

on both sides attended a handover ceremony in December 1982, and a larger ribbon-cutting celebration was held the following month featuring Togo's President Gnassingbé Eyadéma. In 1985, China's government signed an agreement to provide an interest-free loan and construct Ghana's National Theater (加纳国家剧院). The theater project broke ground in August 1990 and was completed and handed over two years later in 1992. China's government also financed and built a CNY50 million Kathmandu International Conference Center (加德满都国际会议大厦) agreed upon in 1987. Over the same period, China remained active in constructing national stadiums in the Global South. Kenyan president Daniel arap Moi visited China in 1980 and requested a national sports center. The two countries signed an Agreement on Economic and Technical Cooperation in September and a protocol for the Nairobi Athletic Complex. After a series of follow-up agreements, construction on the Moi International Sports Center (莫伊国际体育中心), shown in Figure 7, began in December 1982 and cost roughly US$52 million, most of which was provided through interest-free loans. The first phase was completed in 1987 and handed over in time for the All-Africa Games later that year.

High-profile infrastructure also remained as a component of Chinese development finance through the end of the twentieth century. For example, China financed and built the Thanlyin Bridge (仰光—丁茵大桥) in Myanmar connecting the city of Thanlyin to the former capital of Yangon. Construction on

Figure 7 Moi international sports center (莫伊国际体育中心)
Source: The Standard.

Myanmar's first major bridge began in 1986 and finished in July 1993 – pictured in Figure 8 – after encountering delays caused by nationwide political instability and protests during Myanmar's 1988 Uprising. It was one of China's largest overseas road projects at the time and was implemented by China Railway Major Bridge Engineering Group (中铁大桥局).

Some of these examples highlight that China's government has financed global infrastructure where other donors and lenders refused to. But this certainly does not imply that the Chinese government, historically or during the current period, accepts all project requests it receives from other countries. For instance, as China tempered its revolutionary foreign aid strategy and adjusted its regional foreign policy priorities during the 1970s, "requests from West Africa, like the railway between Guinea and Mali or the potentially profitable Manantali Dam in the Senegal River basin, were systematically rejected" (Lorenzini 2019, 116). China's government does not accept all requests it receives for high-profile infrastructure today, either. China Eximbank has backed out of multiple rail projects in recent years, such as the modernization of a railway segment between Kaduna and Kano in Nigeria because of concerns about the COVID-19 pandemic, Nigeria's ability to repay, and heightened scrutiny of Chinese rail projects in the country.[36] Host countries too, of course, can walk away from potential global infrastructure projects, and this has occurred at times during the first decade of the BRI (e.g. Dourado 2023). Nor do all initial agreements come to fruition. Many historical and contemporary project proposals have failed to make

---

[36] www.scmp.com/news/china/diplomacy/article/3216391/china-making-cautious-return-african-infrastructure-funding.

Figure 8 Thanlyin bridge (仰光–丁茵大桥)
Source: Embassy of the People's Republic of China in Myanmar.

it past initial negotiation and commitment stages. For instance, China, Mali, and Senegal in 1968 agreed to finance a 360-km cross-border railway providing maritime access to Mali, but the project, previously dismissed by Mali's French colonial rulers, stalled after Senegal backed out (Bräutigam 2019a).

To summarize, carefully defining and measuring Chinese global infrastructure reveals an important project class that has been a tenacious cornerstone of China's development finance program. The relative salience of these projects has shifted at times – rising, for example, during China's revolutionary foreign policy, and declining during the early reform and opening period – but the Chinese government has continuously financed and constructed high-profile and prestige infrastructure projects across the Global South amid shifting political and economic priorities. In aggregate, perhaps no other donor or creditor has been as consistent in their willingness to fund and build global infrastructure. As the following section discusses, the political attraction of global infrastructure, both for the governments of host countries and the Chinese government, helps explain this tenacity.

4 The Infrastructure-Influence Nexus

Contemporary economic goals alone cannot explain Chinese global infrastructure given its twentieth-century pedigree. This section turns to the political dynamics of Chinese global infrastructure, with a particular focus on China's pursuit of international influence. It first examines policy and academic debates about infrastructure and influence. It then outlines several links between the two, and conceives of global infrastructure as unique political capital – relative to other international development projects – that produces both intended and unintended influence outcomes for China's government.

4.1 Roads to Influence?

Chinese global infrastructure has alarmed the United States and other liberal democracies concerned with Beijing's growing global clout. The suggestion that global infrastructure potentially generates influence is not farfetched.[37] A large literature on the political economy of development finance shows that donor and creditor governments supply development finance – including infrastructure – to pursue influence and reap economic, diplomatic, and geopolitical benefits (e.g. Maizels and Nissanke 1984; Meernik, Krueger, and Poe 1998; Burnside and Dollar 2000). As mentioned in Section 2.2.1, the Chinese government is no exception to this larger pattern in international politics.

Moreover, infrastructure projects were important influence-seeking nodes for donors in earlier eras. Both before and after World War II, a variety of powerful states invested in transportation infrastructure in colonies and newly independent developing countries to project military and logistical power (e.g. Khalili 2021). Throughout much of the Cold War, major powers competed for influence in developing countries by financing and building high-profile infrastructure. The USSR, United States, and China all invested in such projects overseas (e.g. Westad 2005; Latham 2011; Mertha 2014; Engerman 2018; Lorenzini 2019). Powerful states, including Israel, Japan, Russia, and the United Kingdom, also funded and built prestige projects across the Global South during the twentieth century. More recently, "emerging" donors and lenders such as India, Qatar, and Saudi Arabia have begun to finance high-profile and prestige projects during the twenty-first century, and the Chinese government is now the largest provider of these projects (Strange 2023b).

Research on China's infrastructure-influence nexus has sometimes made strong claims. One study, for example, argues that China's government envisions the BRI as "an integrated and interconnected Eurasian continent with enduring authoritarian political systems, where China's influence has grown to the point it has muted any opposition and gained acquiescence and deference" (Rolland 2017, 137). One book claims that "Whoever is able to build

---

[37] Beyond visible, site-specific physical infrastructure, financial and other forms of infrastructure are also important for influence-seeking (de Goede and Westermeier 2022).

and control the infrastructure linking the two ends of Eurasia will rule the world," and that "investment, infrastructure and trade can be used as leverage to shape relations with other countries even more in its favor" (Maçães 2018, 3, 30). Another recent monograph is even more explicit in linking infrastructure to influence, declaring that "We are in the midst of a *global infrastructure war*" and that China is "'weaponizing' infrastructure by creating a nexus of road, rail, and sea connections spanning half the world to secure prosperity-enhancing trade and investment opportunities and to project both hard (economic) and soft (cultural) power in the process" (Rowley 2020, xxii, 1; emphasis added).[38]

For the most part, however, such claims are anecdotal and underspecified. They are not accompanied by careful conceptualization or measurement needed to assess whether and how global infrastructure generates influence. Other recent research treats the infrastructure-influence nexus more carefully. Ho (2020) suggests that Chinese infrastructure in Southeast Asia wields both structural power and discursive power. Hillman (2019a, 2) specifies twelve influence functions across three stages of financing, design and build, and ownership and operation, from buying policy concessions to collecting intelligence. Others highlight potential security implications of specific types of Chinese-owned or operated overseas infrastructure such as maritime ports (Kardon and Leutert 2022), government buildings (Meservey 2020), or surveillance systems (Greitens 2020). Lampton, Ho, and Kuik (2020) and Ho (2020) examine China's use of rail infrastructure to exercise different forms of influence, including structural dependence, narrative control, military access, and economic integration.

A growing chorus of scholars have additionally pointed out that Chinese influence hinges on host country factors, not simply what China desires or does. Hillman (2020)'s study focuses on infrastructure along the BRI and points out that the success of BRI infrastructure also depends on choices made by host country governments.[39] Studies such as Lampton, Ho, and Kuik (2020) and Wong (2021) similarly show that host agency – manifested through popular and elite opinion and contestation, domestic political institutions, civil society organizations, and so on – fundamentally shapes BRI infrastructure

---

[38] Others claim that specific forms of global infrastructure, such as China's overseas high-speed rail, "provides a powerful means to project broader political influence and deepen bilateral ties" (Ker 2017, 3).

[39] Though it also suggests that China can largely control the BRI's contribution to its power, which "hinges on China having the discipline to choose the right projects and walk away from the wrong ones" (Hillman 2020, 14).

negotiations, implementation, and reception, as well as the influence consequences for China.

All of this research is a helpful start, but most existing studies emphasize global infrastructure's deliberate, positive influence potential while ignoring or downplaying its risks. It focuses heavily on efforts by the Chinese government and envisions scenarios in which China, the influence-seeker, purposefully wields influence over smaller states through global infrastructure negotiations and implementation. While some existing studies acknowledge the risks of global infrastructure for Chinese influence, few carefully study them.[40] As the following sections discuss, global infrastructure's distinctive attributes relative to other development projects – discussed in Section 3 – complicate how these projects actually affect China's influence.

4.2 Clarifying Influence Outcomes

Clearer definitions are needed for linking infrastructure to influence. Having conceptualized global infrastructure in Section 3, this section turns to different types of influence that states desire in international politics. Much like "infrastructure," "influence" has often been deployed as a nebulous, catch-all term when discussing the BRI. Influence is traditionally defined in political science as an actor's ability to change another actor's behavior in ways that reflect its own desires and in ways that the other actor would not otherwise choose (e.g. Dahl 1984). However, in the context of global infrastructure, a more inclusive, multilayered conceptualization is better equipped to document different influence processes and outcomes (e.g. Goh 2014; Kastner and Pearson 2021; Fung et al. 2023).

As a starting point, global infrastructure, and development finance more generally, can be used to pursue least two general types of influence outcomes.[41] First, it can generate "elite influence," or state-level outcomes that support the donor or lender's national interests (e.g. Bueno de Mesquita and Smith 2007; Bueno de Mesquita and Smith 2009; Dreher, Sturm, and Vreeland 2009; Dreher et al. 2018). In the context of international development, elite influence has generally referred to policy concessions or other high-level, state-to-state influence outcomes. Elite influence is also the primary outcome that many studies have examined in the context of Chinese "economic statecraft." For instance, using a variety of data sources, earlier research finds that China can secure influence in the form of UNGA or UNSC votes, or diplomatic

---

[40] For example, Hillman (2019a; 2020) mentions unintended influence consequences, but primarily focuses on deliberate channels by which China pursues influence.

[41] This paragraph draws on Strange (Forthcoming).

solidarity on various domestic and international political issues, by providing economic carrots to other countries (e.g. Flores-Macias and Kreps 2013; Kastner 2016). Elite influence hinges on the behavior of national leaders of countries that host infrastructure projects.

In addition, infrastructure and other projects can be used to pursue "popular influence" that enables donors and lenders to accumulate "soft power" and win "hearts and minds" among foreign audiences by demonstrating generosity, competence, or other desirable attributes (Berman, Shapiro, and Felter 2011; Goldsmith, Horiuchi, and Wood 2014; Dietrich, Mahmud, and Winters 2018; Blair, Marty, and Roessler 2022; Wellner et al. Forthcoming).[42] Popular influence refers to changes in foreign public opinion that can translate into elite-level policy outcomes that support states' economic, political, or security interests. Like elite influence, popular influence is an important outcome for states' security, political, and economic interests (e.g. Goldsmith and Horiuchi 2012), and states thus care deeply about accumulating it in other countries (Owen 2010; Allan, Vucetic, and Hopf 2018; Brazys and Dukalskis 2019). This is one reason why development organizations spend large sums on highly visible projects and also invest millions of dollars in branding – i.e. labelling, displaying, publicizing, or otherwise communicating – their international development activities to citizens of other countries (Dietrich, Mahmud, and Winters 2018).[43] Visibility matters for popular influence-seeking because it increases the likelihood that individuals will be aware of a project in the first place, making it easier for them to accurately associate the project with different actors.[44] Compared to other development projects, highly visible global infrastructure is thus particularly likely to affect a donor or creditor's popular influence by either improving or hurting its image among foreign publics.

4.3 How Global Infrastructure Helps China Pursue Influence

Global infrastructures are arguably China's most consequential development projects for questions of influence. Both the sheer size and political salience of these projects make global infrastructure politically valuable both for host country governments and for donors and lenders seeking elite or popular influence.

---

[42] Soft power is usually defined as governments' ability to advance their interests via "co-optation and attraction rather than exclusively through coercion," and favorable foreign public opinion is a common measure of soft power (e.g., Nye 2004; Goldsmith and Horiuchi 2012).

[43] Major donors like the United States Agency for International Development (USAID) and counterpart agencies of other OECD members actively brand their aid (Moore 2018), as do "emerging" donors and lenders including China (Rudyak 2019b).

[44] This should not be taken for granted, as available evidence shows that observers often have incomplete information on development project actors (e.g. Baldwin and Winters 2020).

4.3.1 Global Infrastructure as National Political Capital

Global infrastructure helps support Chinese influence-seeking in part because it is politically useful to host country governments that acquire it. It is thus useful to first consider how global infrastructure's visibility and national salience create political opportunity for host governments. It is well-established in political economy research that delivering visible infrastructure and other projects can sometimes benefit politicians domestically. Politicians at various levels of government thus often have political incentives to pursue domestically financed infrastructure and other visible development projects (Mani and Mukand 2007; Harding 2015; Lei and Zhou 2022). For governments unable to finance major infrastructure projects internally, international development capital offers otherwise available opportunities. For example, host country leaders can sometimes use foreign aid projects to bolster their own political authority, especially when these projects are highly visible (Briggs 2012; Weghorst and Lindberg 2013; Cruz and Schneider 2017; Marx 2018).

Global infrastructure projects offer major potential as national-level economic and political capital for host country leaders. These projects are potentially politically useful for a number of reasons. Governments can acquire externally financed infrastructure projects and brand them as national achievements, allowing them to claim credit for major economic development initiatives and pursue higher support among relevant domestic audiences. In addition to the promise of economic development, global infrastructure enables host country leaders to pursue a variety of additional strategic goals. Though public infrastructure is typically viewed as a public good, some infrastructures also allow states to provide patronage to politically important constituents, and this is one explanation for why countries like Ghana and Zambia, to name but two, have historically invested in socioeconomically questionable projects (e.g. Robinson and Torvik 2005). Other infrastructure projects can facilitate the extension of material power at home by enhancing the state's capacity in various policy domains as well as its territorial reach throughout the country (Herbst 2000, 42; Guldi 2012). Infrastructure – including both administrative and physical structures – is thus an important tool for statebuilding and increasing the state's monopoly on domestic resources and power (e.g. Mann 1984; Tilly 1990; Centeno 2002). Externally financed infrastructure that serves these functions can similarly provide host country governments with additional capital for enhancing state authority.

Global infrastructure can also possess symbolic value for host states in addition to material functions. Large infrastructure projects can play nationally symbolic roles as "objects of imagination, vision, and hope" (Müller-Mahn, Mkutu, and Kioko 2021). As an example, Pakistan's government financed hydroelectric power stations and a new capital city during the 1960s that demonstrated the government's power and transmitted "national imageries," and more recently has invested in urban infrastructure projects such as rapid transit systems in part to provide imagery and showcase performative infrastructure that reflects "world class" aspirations (Sajjad and Javed 2022, 1498–1499). As Larkin (2018) explains, the political value of infrastructure operates materially – for instance, by delivering economic value or physically increasing a government's ruling capacity – as well as aesthetically, by engaging individuals and communities.[45] Governments and leaders who can provide symbolic, national-level projects may hope to bolster their standing among relevant elite or popular audiences.

Alternatively, they may be able to use global infrastructures to exercise symbolic power – generally conceptualized by Bourdieu (1991) as the act of constructing or reinforcing perceived political or social realities – by aggressively branding them during important project milestones and associating projects with their own political authority (Steinberg 1987). Global infrastructure projects, though financed and built by foreign actors, can allow leaders to acquire and convey national political symbols. This makes global infrastructure politically valuable for governments relative to other development projects, and situates them in a broader phenomenon of states' strategic use of symbolic and performative tools (e.g. Bourdieu 1991; Wedeen 2015; Ding 2020).

Another possibility is that infrastructure offers otherwise unavailable opportunities to pursue regional or international status. Acquiring prestige projects could lead to a sense of enhanced status by prompting regime elites or citizens to positively evaluate their nation relative to neighboring or other countries (Frank 1985). This can be an important motivator for states' investment in large visible infrastructure. For example, Ethiopia's recent investment in conspicuous, luxury infrastructure in urban areas such as palaces, parks, and residences appears to be part of a bid to increase its regional status by targeting domestic elites, Ethiopian diaspora communities, and foreigners (Terrefe 2020; Gebreluel 2023). In the context of prestige projects, for instance, securing the region's newest and most modern entertainment venue, convention center, or football stadium may be perceived by both leaders and members of the public as a status-changing development.

---

[45] Infrastructures "are made up of desire as much as concrete or steel and to separate off these dimensions is to miss out on the powerful ways they are consequential for our world" (Larkin 2018, 176).

Both historical and contemporary Chinese global infrastructures display many of these functions. For example, both historically and in recent years, host country leaders have secured Chinese-financed prestige infrastructure in the lead-up to regionally important events. For example, In the late 1950s China's government agreed to finance and build a sports facility for Cambodia as it prepared to host the Asian Games of the Games of New Emerging Forces (GANEFO). Over fifty years later, China again assisted Cambodia with a stadium after Prime Minister Hun Sen requested it in 2014 in preparation for hosting the 2023 Southeast Asian Games. China completed Morodok Techo National Stadium, a US$169-million project, in December 2021 after four years of work.

As shown in Section 3.4, autocratic governments are not the only regimes interested in Chinese global infrastructure. In March 2009, for instance, Costa Rica's government held a groundbreaking ceremony for a new 35,000-seat national stadium (displayed in Figure 9). It cost over $100 million and was completed in March 2011 after China's government financed and built the project. For Costa Rica's government, the arena was an important source of national political capital. It enabled them to deliver a national-level landmark that would be highly visible to domestic and international audiences. Costa Rican President Óscar Arias was eager to bolster Costa Rica's international standing and requested for China's government to provide the stadium while in Beijing for a state visit during October 2007. After the project was initiated, Costa Rica's government utilized key moments to brand the stadium as a central achievement of both the country and the government (DeHart 2012; Verri 2020).

Figure 9 National stadium of Costa Rica (哥斯达黎加国家体育场)
Source: Central South Architectural Design Institute.

In short, global infrastructure projects offer national leaders of developing countries otherwise unavailable opportunities to acquire, deploy, and brand high-visibility, nationally salient projects. These symbolic projects have a variety of economic and political functions, which make them valuable sources of political capital both for host countries. A growing crop of research highlights the domestic political value of Chinese-financed infrastructure projects for host country leaders seeking political security and legitimation at home (e.g. Dreher et al. 2019; Kuik 2021; Wang 2022).[46] Their domestic political value also makes global infrastructures useful for China's international interests.

4.3.2 Global Infrastructure and Elite Influence

China's government can sometimes convert global infrastructure into elite influence, such as political support by host country governments. Global infrastructure projects are useful for elite influence-seeking because they typically directly involve national leaders from host countries. Consider the examples of sports stadiums mentioned earlier. China granted the request for Costa's Rica's national stadium during its pursuit of diplomatic influence vis-à-vis Costa Rica. The national stadium was the "crown jewel" of a larger package given to Costa Rica in exchange for abandoning diplomatic relations with Taiwan, and Beijing agreed to grant and build the stadium a few months after Costa Rica severed diplomatic ties with Taipei in June 2007. This particular instance is emblematic of China's longstanding approach of using global infrastructure and other development projects to establish and bolster political allegiances (Kao 1988). Similarly, Cambodia's aforementioned national stadiums are two of several prestige infrastructure projects that have helped China's government secure Cambodia's consistent diplomatic support over several decades (see Tables A1 and A2).

Donors and lenders regularly use development finance to pursue policy concessions and other elite influence outcomes, and the sheer size of global infrastructure – particularly high-profile projects – may make them especially consequential for securing influence over host states. China's global infrastructure has indeed been linked to Chinese influence-seeking since the Mao era. A prime example is China's successful campaign to unseat Taiwan and claim China's permanent seat at the United Nations in 1971. Table 3 documents China's provision of global infrastructure projects to UN member states who participated in United Nations General Assembly Resolution 2758, through which the PRC was recognized as the sole legitimate representative

---

[46] As discussed below, however, there is little consensus over whether this exercise systematically translates into increased elite or popular support of leaders.

Table 3 Chinese global infrastructure allocation to voting countries on United Nations General Assembly Resolution 2758 (October 1971)

Period	In favor (pro-PRC)	Against (pro-ROC)	Abstain
1966–1971	Afghanistan (1), Albania (9), Algeria (2), Burma (2), Ceylon (2), Equatorial Guinea (1), Ethiopia (2), Guinea (7), Mali (3), Mauritania (3), Nepal (3), Pakistan (4), People's Democratic Republic of Yemen (4), Sierra Leone (6), Somalia (5), Sudan (1), Syrian Arab Republic (1), United Republic of Tanzania (4), Zambia (2)	Khmer Republic (2)	
1972–1977	Afghanistan (2), Albania (2), Burundi (3), Cameroon (3), Ceylon (1), Equatorial Guinea (2), Ethiopia (2), Ghana (1), Guyana (2), Iraq (1), Laos (2), Mali (2), Morocco (1), Nepal (9), Pakistan (1), People's Democratic Republic of Yemen (1), People's Republic of the Congo (3), People's Democratic Republic of Yemen (1), Rwanda (3), Senegal (3), Sierra	Chad (1), Dahomey (1), Upper Volta (1), Congo DRC (3), Gambia (1), Madagascar (5), Malta (5)	Jamaica (1), Mauritius (1)

Table 3 (cont.)

Period	In favor (pro-PRC)	Against (pro-ROC)	Abstain
	Leone (2), Sudan (6), Syrian Arab Republic (3), Tunisia (1), Uganda (1), United Republic of Tanzania (1), Yemen (7), Zambia (2)		

Source: Strange (2023a) and United Nations Digital Library (General Assembly, 26th session: 1976th plenary meeting, Monday, October 25, 1971, New York). Only low- and middle-income developing countries are included in the table. The figures in the table include both high-profile and prestige global infrastructure projects. The numbers in the table are based on committed projects or, in case a specific commitment date is not available, project start or completion dates.

of China to the UN.[47] In the years leading up to the vote, China's government committed global infrastructure projects to over fifteen states that would subsequently vote in its favor. One high-profile project financed during this period was the Vau i Dejës Hydroelectric Power Station in northeast Albania. Albania initially led the sponsorship of the resolution and was a major socialist ally and recipient of Chinese development finance during 1960s. The station, agreed upon in 1967, was commissioned in 1973 and reportedly provided more than half of Albania's electricity at the time.

Similarly, in the years following the resolution, over twenty-five states who voted in favor of the PRC received global infrastructure. One example is the Moukoukoulou Dam, a hydroelectric power station China helped the Republic of Congo build along the Bouenza River beginning in the fall of 1974. It was officially completed in 1979 and became the country's largest hydroelectric power source at the time. Seven states who voted against China also received global infrastructure. In nearly all cases, these were governments who had subsequently severed diplomatic ties with Taiwan. One such project was the aforementioned Moramanga-Andranonampango highway in Madagascar, which was agreed upon in 1975 after Antananarivo ended its official relations with Taipei a few years earlier.

---

[47] This of course is not definitive evidence that global infrastructure shaped voting outcomes. It is simply an illustration of the potential association between voting and infrastructure acquisition before and after the resolution.

Prestige projects are also important for China's elite influence-seeking, particularly in small states in the Global South such as the aforementioned examples of Cambodia and Costa Rica. My analysis of several hundred prestige projects financed by China since the 1950s finds that countries who abandon diplomatic recognition of Taiwan are disproportionately more likely to acquire a Chinese-financed prestige project in the following year (Strange 2023b).

Elite influence such as high-level diplomatic support is only one potential influence outcome that Chinese global infrastructure can produce. The same projects can provide a myriad of other economic, political, or security benefits for Chinese official or commercial actors. For example, infrastructure projects that make use of Chinese industrial inputs produced in excess often mandate that host countries procure construction materials from Chinese companies. Chinese SOEs can sometimes enjoy preferential treatment in procurement processes, particularly in noncompetitive host country industries (e.g. Lim 2014; Ghossein, Hoekman, and Shingal 2018). China's overseas development projects can also serve as sites of long-term relational capital building that helps Chinese commercial actors increase their future investments in developing countries (Morgan and Zheng 2019).

4.3.3 Global Infrastructure and Popular Influence

Global infrastructure may also be useful for China's pursuit of popular influence in developing countries. As mentioned earlier, donors and lenders spend significant resources promoting their generosity to accumulate favorable standing among foreign audiences. On the one hand, global infrastructure may be especially well-suited for promoting China's image as the largest, most visible projects in China's overseas development finance portfolio. The Chinese government has a reputation for mobilizing resources and producing large-scale infrastructure efficiently at home, and has built a parallel reputation in the field of global development. Rotberg (2009, 75) notes that "High-profile construction projects, such as building resplendent stadia to house national football teams," have been effective at both "sweetening popular perceptions" of China and cementing relations with African governments "which take credit for having negotiated China's contributions to national development – the same efforts that some African leaders have been unable or unwilling to undertake on their own."

On the other hand, popular influence depends on the reactions of target audiences, and not simply the messages that donor or lender governments hope to convey. Systematic public opinion data toward historical Chinese development projects is not available. But evidence sourced from around the world over the first decade of the BRI, if anything, suggests that public attitudes toward Chinese global infrastructure are deeply mixed (e.g. Custer et al. 2015; Lekorwe et al. 2016), and initial academic evidence paints a similar picture. Table 4 lists several recent studies focused on host country popular attitudes toward different forms of Chinese development cooperation, primarily its development finance projects. Overall the results are mixed: Different articles using different data sources, measures, and study contexts find negative, positive, or null effects of Chinese development projects on attitudes toward China's government. The table also shows that few studies directly investigate perceptions of Chinese infrastructure, though several include relevant findings, and that much of this research has thus far been conducted using surveys administered in African countries.

In summary, infrastructure can serve as a deliberate means for China to pursue elite and popular influence, though there is less evidence of success for the latter. However, global infrastructure can also generate unforeseen and potentially unwanted influence consequences that have received comparatively less attention in earlier research.

4.4 Influence Externalities

Global infrastructure can also activate unintentional influence processes and outcomes. Unintended consequences have received less popular and scholarly attention than China's deliberate influence efforts. Political scientists have long argued that certain forms of power and influence occur unintentionally (see, for instance, Barnett and Duvall 2005 and Lukes 2005). This section suggests that Chinese high-profile infrastructure (and prestige infrastructure, to a lesser extent) often produce "influence externalities" for China's government. Influence externalities are changes to a state's international influence that occur unintentionally and independently of the state's objectives due to changes in behavior or perceptions by foreign state or non-state actors.[48] Intuitively, though visibility and national salience make global infrastructure initially attractive for the host country government and for China's government, the same features also create and amplify unintentional influence consequences.

The suggestion that infrastructure creates unintended consequences is certainly not new. Research in other fields documents how infrastructure generates unexpected economic, social, political, and environmental outcomes (e.g. Scott 1998; Li 2007; Guldi 2012). Compared to other development activities, global infrastructure is uniquely visible and politically salient within host countries, and these features make it an enticing but risky source of national political

---

[48] This concept is somewhat analogous to security externalities generated from interstate trade (Gowa and Mansfield 1993).

Table 4 Selected recent findings on Chinese infrastructure-related flows and popular influence in developing countries

Study	Chinese activity	Outcome	Findings	Region	Infrastructure-relevant notes
Morgan (2019)	Various (exports, aid, investment)	Image of China; Evaluation of China's development assistance; Attitudes toward China's influence	Mixed; positive for aid	Sub-Saharan Africa	Aid and infrastructure associated with positive evaluations
Xu and Zhang (2020)	Development projects	Evaluation of China's development assistance	Positive	Sub-Saharan Africa	Results strongest for infrastructure-heavy sectors
Blair, Marty, and Roessler (2022)	Development projects	Attitudes toward China's influence; belief that China's model is best	Negative	Sub-Saharan Africa	Results strongest for infrastructure-heavy sectors
Eichenauer et al. (2021)	Various (exports, aid, investment)	Opinion of China (good or bad)	Null (but increase in polarized attitudes)	Latin America	N/A

Study	Project type	Outcome	Direction	Region	Notes
Jones (2021)	Development projects	Attitudes toward China's influence; belief that China's model is best	Negative	Sub-Saharan Africa	Results strongest for commercially-oriented projects
Bai, Li, and Wang (2022)	Development projects	Support for Chinese values	Positive	Global	Results strongest for infrastructure-oriented projects
Cha, Ryoo, and Kim (2023)	Development projects and cultural diplomacy	Attitudes toward China's influence; belief that China's model is best	Mixed; null for development projects	Sub-Saharan Africa	Exposure to development projects associated with viewing infrastructure investment as contributing to China's positive image
McCauley, Pearson, and Wang (2022)	Foreign direct investment (FDI) projects	Attitudes toward China's influence; belief that China's model is best	Negative	Sub-Saharan Africa	Manufacturing projects lead respondents to attribute infrastructure improvements to China
Wellner et al. (Forthcoming)	Development projects	Approval of China's leadership	Positive	Global	Results strongest for concessional and large projects

capital. Outsized presence "is why infrastructures are often objects around which political debates coalesce," and the grand promises offered by global infrastructure make these projects "reflexive points where the present state and future possibilities of government and society are held up for public assessment" (Larkin 2018, 177). Global infrastructure is contentious, and different local, national, and international actors interpret and contest its multidimensional costs and benefits.[49]

It is even less controversial to suggest that overseas infrastructure is risky. The history of infrastructure and global development is replete with examples of unintended outcomes, including project failures with negative economic and noneconomic consequences for funders and implementers. In the early twentieth century, state-encouraged private investments in infrastructure projects across the Global South by American companies like General Electric often proved volatile and unprofitable (Wells and Gleason 1995). Global infrastructure has a similarly controversial track record in postwar international development. For example, large infrastructure projects financed by the World Bank – now often portrayed as a bearer of stringent standards that Chinese actors often fail to uphold – have been prone to corruption, delays, and cost increases (e.g. Bissio 2017). World Bank-supported infrastructure has historically been vulnerable to political capture in developing countries (Winters 2014), and this has led to major learnings and adjustments with regards to project design, bidding, and implementation processes (Council on Foreign Relations 2006). The Polonoroeste road project offers an illustration of how the World Bank has encountered adverse unintended consequences, including extremely negative publicity, as the result of a high-profile project. The road project resulted in significant environmental damage and fueled corruption in the Amazon, and contributed to the worsening of the World Bank's reputation (Wade 2016).

Other major donors and creditors have also encountered negative, unintended consequences stemming from global infrastructure projects. Today Japanese development finance is often portrayed as a model of high-quality infrastructure financing and construction. But during the 1980s Japanese infrastructure contractors became implicated in a major corruption scandal that embarrassed Japan's government and led to major policy reforms for overseas development finance (Hillman 2019b). South Korea's overseas infrastructure projects have also become entangled in unexpected controversy. In 2016 it became publicly known that President Park Geun-hye's influential friend and advisor, Choi Soon-sil, was potentially using an ODA-financed

---

[49] Indeed, an entire book has been written in which three authors disagree on the nature and impacts of Chinese-financed projects in developing countries (Bunkenborg, Nielsen, and Pederson 2022).

infrastructure project – a convention center in Myanmar – for personal benefit (Kim 2018). The scandal contributed to widespread negative sentiment towards Park, who was eventually impeached. Put simply, negative unintended consequences are not a unique challenge for the BRI or Chinese global infrastructure.

That said, the raw scale of contemporary Chinese global infrastructure far exceeds that of other major financiers, and influence externalities have occurred frequently and widely across the BRI during its first decade. In what follows, I outline two interrelated processes – political mobilization and narratives – that have frequently coalesced around Chinese global infrastructure projects and created influence consequences for China's government. This of course is not meant as an exhaustive menu for how infrastructure creates unintended outcomes, but as an illustration of two important processes that complicate the relationship between infrastructure and influence.[50]

4.4.1 Host Country Political Mobilization

Global infrastructure projects provide visible symbols around which state or non-state actors can mobilize to pursue project-specific or grander objectives in host countries. As mentioned earlier, national leaders are often first movers in this regard. They request, negotiate, acquire, and brand global infrastructure as important national projects. But mobilization by other actors has repeatedly taken both host governments and China's government by surprise, and in some cases has impacted China's foreign policy influence.

Mobilization has often emerged as projects move from negotiations to implementation. Infrastructure is often negotiated directly between national-level governments and thus tends to be relatively insulated from input by local communities, civil society organizations (CSOs) and nongovernmental organizations (NGOs), opposition parties, and other domestic actors, even in relatively democratic settings (e.g. Flyvbjerg et al. 2003). Chinese high-profile and prestige infrastructure conforms to this general pattern, and might even magnify this discord if negotiations with host country governments are highly opaque and shielded from other domestic and international audiences in ways that allow host governments to initially avoid accountability and scrutiny.

The first decade of the BRI has shown that initially bypassing domestic stakeholders can make it more likely that these actors will later mobilize and disrupt infrastructure projects. Researchers have documented numerous

---

[50] Others have argued, for instance, that Chinese high-profile infrastructure projects can affect China's influence in unexpected ways due to each country's level of patience and availability of potential alternative options (Oh 2018).

examples of mobilization around Chinese global infrastructure by local, regional, or national groups to pursue and defend their interests related to economic, labor, and environmental issues. Mobilization has emerged through both bottom-up and top-down processes that have created influence external-ities for China.

On the one hand, Chinese high-profile infrastructure has generated strong grassroots reactions among locally affected stakeholders. One prominent recent example is Kenya's Lamu Coal Power Plant. After several high-ranking Kenyan cabinet officials first announced it as a strategic national project, local CSOs spent several years publicly campaigning against the plant, citing concerns of pollution and environmental degradation (Kinney 2022). Bottom-up mobiliza-tion succeeded when the project was cancelled in 2019.[51] CSOs and labor groups in Zambia have similarly found success in mobilizing to oppose poten-tially problematic Chinese infrastructure projects. This changed international negotiation dynamics between Zambia and China, potentially affecting China's bargaining power and ability to generate elite influence (Leslie 2016).

The suspended Myitsone Dam in Myanmar, which possesses important eco-nomic and latent geostrategic value for China's government, is another oft-cited example of how local stakeholders mobilized in ways that shifted China's influ-ence. It was initially negotiated by Myanmar's military junta beginning in 2006 with little input or opposition allowed by other domestic actors. But after Myanmar's temporary democratization in 2011, public mobilization efforts led by a coalition of conservationists, media figures, CSOs, academics, and activists popularized an anti-dam campaign citing concerns of socioeconomic disruption to communities in Kachin State as well as environmental and social harm along the Irrawaddy River. Myanmar's government unilaterally suspended the dam, but China did not retaliate against Myanmar's breach of contract. Instead, perceiving Myanmar's domestic opposition as credible, China's government sought to increase local buy-in to the dam and renegotiate it on more favorable terms to these affected groups (Chan 2017). The fates of other Chinese high-profile projects in Myanmar, including the halted China-Myanmar High-Speed Railway, similarly suggest that host country mobilization can circumscribe China's ability to shape government-to-government negotiations (Chan 2020). China's popular influence in host countries can also increase or decrease as a result of domestic mobilizations, which might further constrain its influence over future negotiations for other projects or bilateral issues.

Mobilization around Chinese global infrastructure can also operate through high-level actors who engage with domestic public audiences. This infamously occurred

---

[51] www.bbc.com/news/world-africa-48771519.

in 2018 when Malaysian Prime Minister Mahathir Mohamad, elected again as prime minister after serving decades earlier, cancelled over $20 billion in Chinese high-profile infrastructure projects signed by his predecessor, Najib Razak. Multiple high-profile projects became embroiled in highly public corruption scandals and amid mounting debt to China. These included the East Coast Rail Link (ECRL, pictured in Figure 10) and Bandar Malaysia, a mixed development housing project in Kuala Lumpur (Liu and Lim 2019).

The ECRL illustrates how high-level political actors in host countries can produce influence externalities for China. The railway was envisioned by Malaysian and Chinese leaders as a flagship national project. At the time of negotiation, the Razak-led Malaysian government viewed the ECRL as a landmark project that could stimulate growth and reduce inequality between Malaysia's politically important but economically underdeveloped east coast states and the more prosperous Selangor state. For China, in addition to the project's commercial value, the rail would also deliver geostrategic benefits as an alternate transportation corridor to the Strait of Malacca (Lim, Li, and Ji 2022). However, opposition groups led by Mahathir attacked the ECRL and other Chinese high-profile infrastructure on the basis of their opaqueness and lack of competitive tenders for construction. Upon entering office for a second time as prime minister, Mahathir infamously deferred the ECRL during a 2018 trip to Beijing. Less than a year later, he renegotiated the ECRL on more

Figure 10 East coast rail link (东海岸衔接铁道)
Source: Xinhua.

favorable terms and at a lower cost to Malaysia (Lim, Li, and Ji 2022). The railway is currently under construction.

Over 1,500 km south of Kuala Lumpur, Indonesia offers another example in which a Chinese-supported high-speed rail project has threatened to destabilize China's popular and elite influence. Domestic debates in Indonesia involving Chinese global infrastructure, particularly the recently completed Jakarta–Bandung High Speed Rail (雅万高铁) on the island of Java, have provided important political fodder for Indonesian politicians. Indonesia's leadership has effectively wielded growing popular frustration toward China generally in recent years, some of which stems from the unpopularity of expensive, controversial projects such as the aforementioned high-speed rail link and the Indonesia Morowali Industrial Park, to increase their bargaining power in negotiations with China for future infrastructure projects (Tritto 2020; Camba 2020).

As these brief examples show, global infrastructure provides visible touchpoints for both grassroots and high-level mobilization. In each of these cases, China's government encountered potential influence externalities, primarily in the form of challenges to its ability to negotiate bilaterally, its popular influence in host countries, and the interaction between these elite and popular influence dynamics. Mobilization can also directly affect China's influence when individual projects designed to achieve important economic or political objectives for China have been halted, cancelled, or scaled back because of political mobilization. China's negotiating position for ongoing and planned infrastructure has shifted – and sometimes worsened – relative to counterpart governments whose hands can become credibly tied by domestic audiences. Beyond the aforementioned examples of Indonesia and Myanmar, this has also recently occurred in BRI host countries such as Sri Lanka, Maldives, Papua New Guinea, and Kenya, to name a few.

Available examples suggest that host country mobilization has more often curtailed rather than expanded China's influence. Two caveats are in order, however. First, in some contexts, mobilization dynamics are weaker and appear less threatening to China's interests. In several Central Asian countries, including Kazakhstan, for example, despite souring popular sentiment toward Chinese-financed high-profile infrastructure, there is comparatively less evidence that China's influence has diminished. One factor that may help explain this outcome is China's successful co-optation of local and regional politicians in these countries (Kazantsev, Medvedeva, and Safranchuk 2021; Umarov 2021).

Second, political mobilization is not always based on negative sentiment toward Chinese global infrastructure. In fact, despite strongly negative international rhetoric toward the BRI – particularly in the United States and other Western democracies – elite and popular attitudes in dozens of BRI host countries are considerably more mixed (see 4.3.3). Concerns about debt sustainability, transparency, and accountability notwithstanding, China's specialization in global infrastructure still appears welcome among many audiences in developing countries. Both materially and reputationally, China's government now has a comparative advantage relative to other foreign financiers in building global infrastructure. Cross-national survey evidence shows that officials in African countries tend to view China's government positively in terms of its swift decision-making, project implementation speed, and reluctance to meddle in other state affairs (Shikwati, Adero, and Juma 2022).[52] While troubled BRI projects attract the bulk of mainstream media attention, as highlighted in Section 3, a significant portion of China's high-profile infrastructure is actually completed ahead of schedule and in some cases has helped relieve infrastructure bottlenecks in host countries (e.g. Bräutigam 2019b; Bluhm et al. 2021; Malik et al. 2021).

Host country politicians sometimes highlight these advantages when mobilizing *in favor of* Chinese global infrastructure. Politicians regularly point domestic audiences to visible projects, particularly completed ones. Former Zambian President Edgar Lungu did this during his failed re-election bid in 2020, unveiling a newly built, Chinese-financed hydropower station and two airports just weeks before national elections.[53] During Sierra Leone's 2018 general elections, the incumbent All People's Congress prominently (and ultimately unsuccessfully) highlighted its close relations with China on the campaign trail (Rinck 2019). This was after a decade of Chinese global infrastructure and other development financing in the country, including a promised high-profile airport project that failed to materialize under former president Ernest Bai Koroma.[54]

4.4.2 Narratives

Mobilization is closely related to another process that can unintentionally alter China's influence: the creation and proliferation of infrastructure-related narratives. Narratives can accelerate political mobilization at local, national, or international levels, and amplify resulting influence consequences for China's government. Narratives are a basic feature of political discourse in both official

---

[52] China is also seen as more likely to use corruption to grease the wheels of commerce, less likely to provide high-quality products, and less likely to drive local job creation compared to the European Union.

[53] https://chinaglobalsouth.com/2021/08/05/one-week-to-go-before-the-zambian-elections-and-president-lungu-leans-hard-on-chinese-built-infrastructure/.

[54] After former President Ernest Bai Koroma signed a loan agreement prior to the national election, the new administration cancelled the deal in 2018. See "Mamamah airport: Sierra Leone cancels China-funded project," BBC, October 10, 2018. https://www.bbc.com/news/world-africa-45809810.

news and everyday conversations both offline and on the internet and social media platforms. Researchers have long suggested that narratives, defined most simply as "the stories people tell," shape political attitudes and behavior (Patterson and Monroe 1998).[55] They play a cognitive role in helping people "make sense of our place in the world" and understand complex issues in everyday life (Patterson and Monroe 1998, 319).[56] Narratives "establish the common-sense givens of debate, set the boundaries of the legitimate, limit what political actors inside and outside the halls of power can publicly justify, and resist efforts to remake the landscape of legitimation" (Krebs 2015, 3).

Narratives are important in the context of global infrastructure because they offer a way for people to simplify and make sense of operationally and financially complicated projects. Infrastructure narratives can also serve as vehicles for transmitting or even constituting political symbols, or "schemata that individuals use to simplify a complex world" among elite and popular audiences (Schatz 2021, 6). Political messages that global infrastructure come to represent are shared among individuals in society and can become resources around which actors mobilize. These features make narratives important mediums of contestation in local, national, and international politics alongside the actual infrastructure projects they describe. Infrastructure narratives are thus critical for donors' and lenders' pursuit of elite and popular influence.

Narratives about global infrastructure projects have produced unintended consequences for China's influence. Some of these narratives exist locally and pertain to projects in a single community or region. Others have emerged and spread at scale, becoming national or international topics of discussion that permeate high-level political discourse. In international relations, most of the cases we observe and focus on are the latter: simplistic narratives that have gained traction and affected China's negotiations with other countries as well as Beijing's international reputation. Sri Lanka's Hambantota Port and its central role in the "debt-trap diplomacy" narrative – in which China's government lures developing country governments into heavy debt burdens in order to extract strategic benefits – is the best-known example. But other recent instances, including high-profile infrastructure in Kenya and Malaysia, have also demonstrated how project narratives can proliferate at local, national, and international levels (Bräutigam 2020; Hameiri and Jones 2020; Bräutigam et al. 2023).

---

[55] Bruner (1990, 90) defines a narrative as a "unique sequence of events, mental states, happenings involving human beings as characters or actors" that is often dramatic and can be effective regardless of its empirical accuracy. Narratives are also described as devices to help people make sense of a perceived problem or irregularity (Patterson and Monroe 1998).

[56] As such, narratives, by definition, are subjective and conditioned on what is valued within a social and cultural context.

Two additional features of Chinese global infrastructure – the complex relationship between Chinese state and non-state actors, and the diverse set of Chinese actors operating in developing countries – have affected local, national, and international infrastructure narratives. The first relates to a separate, longstanding principal-agent problem in the context of Chinese global economic engagement that can also fuel the spread of problematic narratives for China. Delegation of strategic responsibilities to quasi- or non-state agents that behave based on their own interests, such as profit-oriented firms operating overseas, has been a consistent challenge for China's government during its global infrastructure drive (Gill and Reilly 2007; Shi 2015; Norris 2016). When these actors behave in ways that stray from China's officially stated interests, this can create new or contribute to existing narratives about Chinese infrastructure.

Across all of China's engagements with developing countries, this principal-agent problem is arguably most severe for large, complex infrastructure projects. Thousands of Chinese state-owned and private companies act as contractors and stakeholders for many of China's high-profile infrastructure projects abroad, and the profit-oriented interests of these actors often do not perfectly align with the interests and intentions of the Chinese state (Sun, Jayaram, and Kassiri 2017; Leutert 2019). The limited ability of China's government to control Chinese commercial actors with global operations further constrains its ability to prevent or manage resulting infrastructure narratives. For example, profit-motivated Chinese SOEs, and especially their local subsidiaries operating in host countries such as Papua New Guinea, can coordinate with host country governments to plan and request infrastructure projects from China's government (Zhang and Smith 2017).[57] Sometimes these projects are based on relatively narrow self-interest rather than host country need or economic feasibility, and are not projects that China's government would otherwise finance.[58] The same projects may include inflated price tags that foster corruption and waste as a result of this coordination. Negative economic or social effects produced as a result can feed into broader narratives that portray China's government as a self-interested, profit-seeking actor rather than a benevolent development partner.

---

[57] In the context of Chinese overseas investments, local Chinese diaspora communities who develop reputations as trustworthy partners for official Chinese actors but pursue their own commercial interests are another potential source of principal-agent problems (Chen 2022).

[58] When Chinese companies with local contextual knowledge and connections are involved with identifying and proposing projects, they may not have incentives to adequately price project risk into proposals, which could lead to suboptimal project selection. In contrast, Chinese policy banks have limited capacity for accurately factoring in risks that arise from local context and need to rely on companies with local operations and presence (Zhang 2020; Patey 2021).

Second, infrastructure narratives are constructed from a wide range of informational inputs from state and non-state actors within and outside host countries. As mentioned earlier, narratives change the information environment and structure available choices for governments and other actors, but their emergence and spread also depends on whether the information they contain is easily understood and consumed by different audiences (e.g. Breuer and Johnston 2019). Creators and distributors of infrastructure narratives simplify extremely financially and operationally complex global infrastructure projects into accessible stories that can be digested by large audiences. In this process of distillation, whether on purpose or accidentally, host country and other actors – whether government bureaucrats, opposition politicians, media organizations, or members of the general public – can easily create misinformation (or disinformation). This in turn can have consequences for China's elite or popular influence, particularly when narratives accelerate host country mobilization.

For example, misattribution of the behavior or identities of quasi- or non-state actors is particularly common in the context of Chinese global infrastructure. Chinese global infrastructure is not provided by a monolithic state but by a complex set of state and quasi-state actors including the central government, various ministries, agencies, and commissions, provincial governments, policy and commercial banks, SOEs, local subsidiaries of Chinese companies, and Chinese managers and workers. Moreover, these infrastructure stakeholders often operate and coexist alongside a diverse set of non-state Chinese actors in many of the same communities in developing countries. For example, in Africa alone, "Chinese investors, shopkeepers, and migrant laborers in Africa are estimated at more than one million people" (Siu and McGovern 2017).[59] Large, diverse populations of overseas Chinese further add to the tapestry of Chinese non-state actors operating in host countries in close proximity to high-profile infrastructure projects (Nyíri and Tan 2017, 16–17). Host-country actors – from ordinary citizens to high-level officials – can accidentally or purposefully misunderstand the nature of China's behavior or misattribute credit or blame to the Chinese government when learning of project successes or failures (e.g. Bräutigam et al. 2022). For example, Peruvians often view both private and state-owned Chinese mining companies operating in their country as being tied to China's government regardless of a company's actual identity (Ratigan 2021).

Of course, misattribution does not only arise in the context of Chinese global infrastructure; donors and lenders routinely face limitations of effectively conveying information about their overseas development projects to foreign

---

[59] Non-state Chinese commercial actors such as petty traders do not simply integrate seamlessly into local societies but operate in complex local environments with preexisting social realities (e.g. Sheridan 2022).

populations. But it seems particularly prevalent for Chinese high-profile infra-structure given these projects' scale, complexity, and coexistence alongside a mosaic of other Chinese state and non-state activities in developing countries. The lack of transparency and disclosure regarding many of China's global high-profile infrastructure projects may further compound this issue.

Importantly, infrastructure-related narratives that are crafted, repackaged, and disseminated by state and non-state actors within and beyond host countries are largely beyond the control of China's government. Many of the sources that contribute to local, national, and global narratives about Chinese infrastructure come from non-Chinese actors. Chinese state actors' viewpoints are inserted into public discourse via media and social media channels, but represent only one input into the production of infrastructure narratives. Misattribution or other informational deficiencies can feed into local or national narratives about China's global infrastructure projects and amplify influence consequences China's government beyond local project sites.

Viewed from this angle, China's contemporary global infrastructure drive is remarkable in the context of a rising China's pursuit of international influence. Over the past decade, the Chinese government has embarked on a major public diplomacy campaign abroad to shore up its global reputation and "tell China's story well" (Caixin 2015). In pursuit of this objective, it has invested billions of dollars in media, social media, storytelling, and cultural exchanges with developing countries that host high-profile infrastructure projects (Brazys and Dukalskis 2019; Benabdallah 2021). But China's efforts to infuse its official perspectives into local discourses outside of China appear to have little sway regarding overall narratives about high-profile infrastructure, which are embedded in local contexts and tied to specific local grievances and stylized interpretations. The fate of infrastructure narratives instead rests more heavily on a complex set of domestic and international actors, and narrative entrepre-neurs who play an outsized role in creating and spreading narratives (Hagstrom and Gustafsson 2019) Global infrastructure, put simply, is a vola-tile tool for popular influence seeking.

In summary, global infrastructure creates influence externalities for China's government. These unintended consequences are an important addendum to earlier accounts that assert China's influence is linearly increasing with its global infrastructure provision. Influence is a net concept that can be gained or lost and decomposed into different layers such as elite and popular outcomes. Many recent examples along the BRI suggest that influence externalities have mostly been negative for China's government in recent years. Host country public reactions to Chinese development activities can produce bottom-up pressures that jeopardize project completion or China's broader strategic interests in a given country or region. Alternatively, opposition politicians in host countries can seize on distressed projects as useful sources of political capital, and not necessarily in ways that help China's influence objectives. Indeed, across the BRI, Chinese-financed projects have occasionally been suspended, mothballed, or cancelled in the face of pressure on host country governments applied by local residents, civil society organizations, and local and national politicians. These mobilizations also depend heavily on infrastructure narratives that, regardless of their empirical veracity or precision, allow local, national, and international audiences to make sense of Chinese global infrastructure. Narratives also provide a political tool for state and non-state actors who, in many cases, utilize narratives about Chinese infrastructure to advance their agendas in ways that affect China's economic or political influence at elite and popular levels. These processes show that China's government has considerably less control over infrastructure-related influence processes and outcomes than other accounts imply.

5 The Past, Present, and Future of Chinese Global Infrastructure

Global infrastructure is one of the defining markers of a more active Chinese foreign policy in recent years. Hundreds of roadways, bridges, railways, airports, harbors, power plants, and factories, along with stadiums, government complexes, and event venues, are among the most prominent symbols of China's presence in the Global South. Within the field of international development, infrastructure is firmly embedded within China's identity as a donor and lender, reflected both through its bilateral global infrastructure projects and its establishment of the AIIB, an explicitly infrastructure-focused multilateral development bank.

However, as the preceding sections demonstrate, Chinese global infrastructure is not a twenty-first-century phenomenon, much less a product of the BRI. Five years into the BRI and shortly after the AIIB was established, the *Economist* (2017) wrote that "China seems to be repeating many of the mistakes made by Western donors and investors in the 1970s" in financing big-ticket infrastructure. This may be true in the sense that risk assessments and economic returns of Chinese global infrastructure are inadequate and uncertain, as was often the case with other lenders' infrastructure development projects. But it neglects that China's global infrastructure lineage predates the 1970s and that China's government has financed and built hundreds of global infrastructure projects in Asia, Africa, and elsewhere across diverse periods of Chinese politics.

Many of China's twenty-first-century global infrastructure projects have encountered stiff local, national, and international criticism, but this is not very surprising when placed in comparative context. Large infrastructure has often performed poorly in terms of speed, efficiency, accountability and corruption control, and net economic benefits. China's state-led approach to global infrastructure has clearly not been immune to these general patterns, neither historically nor in the current era, and certain elements of China's approach may even make negative results more likely. For example, opaque lending terms, inadequate pre-project assessments and safeguards, and direct negotiations with national politicians that can sideline critical voices have all been features, not bugs, within many of China's global infrastructure projects. Still, context is important, and economic problems stemming from these issues are not nearly as distinctive to Chinese global infrastructure as many popular accounts focused only on the BRI might suggest.

However, though *economic* risks of Chinese infrastructure projects are not unique, both the sheer scale of China's post-2000 global infrastructure spree and its historical commitment to global infrastructure since 1949 are remarkable. Hundreds of Chinese global infrastructure projects have injected significant *political* risk that seriously affects China's pursuit of influence. On balance, it appears that global infrastructure has been a useful tool for pursuing elite influence in developing countries via host country governments. In contrast, global infrastructure's effects on China's popular influence, as well as China's long-term net influence, are much less certain.

Global infrastructure's political risks are nonlinear and depend heavily on on-the-ground factors beyond China's control. Chinese global infrastructure has repeatedly encountered contentious domestic mobilization in host countries, often by individuals and groups initially left out of project negotiations. Disruptions caused by mobilization have in some cases altered China's policy interests at the project or national level. They have also affected China's elite and popular influence in developing countries and potentially its international reputation writ large.

Infrastructure narratives have accelerated political mobilization in some cases. Narratives are sometimes contained locally, while other times they spread beyond regional and national borders. Deviations from state goals by Chinese project implementers as well as accidental or purposeful information failures about different Chinese actors can further fuel problematic narratives about Chinese global infrastructure. Collectively, these processes have generated influence externalities beyond China's grasp that modulate – and often imperil – its foreign policy influence in unexpected ways.

Despite this political volatility, the initial political attraction of these ventures for host country governments and the Chinese government is an important reason for their long-term persistence. High-profile and prestige infrastructure have served as valuable forms of political capital given their high visibility and national salience. These features allow global infrastructure projects to perform a host of material and symbolic political functions that other development projects cannot. This makes them useful for host country governments seeking greater political authority at home but unable to fund such projects internally, as well as for the Chinese government's pursuit of international influence.

This Element complements a growing body of research on Chinese development finance heavily fixated on the BRI and financial flows (e.g. Hurley, Morris, and Portelance 2019; Bräutigam 2020; Gelpern et al. 2022; Bräutigam 2022; Horn et al. 2023). Researchers are concerned with Chinese development financial flows for good reason. China's post-2000 global infrastructure drive significantly increased public debt stocks owed to Chinese banks in many developing countries. It has also positioned China's government as one of the most pivotal players in evolving multilateral debt negotiations (Bräutigam 2023). Currently there are also major questions about the future availability of Chinese global infrastructure finance given China's gradually slowing economy, a host of problematic BRI projects and debt-distressed host country governments, and highly publicized BRI "back-lash" in many host countries. Chinese development lending declined sharply before the onset of the pandemic, and it is still unclear to what extent China's government will revive global infrastructure lending in the coming years (Mingey and Kratz 2021; Ray 2023). Citing these trends, along with Chinese bailouts of distressed host governments, some observers appear ready to eulogize the BRI.[60] Others, including China's government, are instead looking to a "recalibrated" BRI featuring more effective risk assessment and a "small is beautiful" (小而美) mentality to project finance.[61]

These are important, future-oriented questions for international relations and development. However, the evidence in this Element suggests that incorporating historical and comparative context allows us to more fully grasp Chinese global infrastructure's historical pedigree and political logics, in addition to its well-known contemporary economic motives and impacts. Chinese global infrastructure's political contours are just as consequential for understanding the persistence of this project class since 1949.

This approach suggests that eulogizing the BRI would not only be premature but also missing the forest for the trees. Many of the contemporary economic objectives as well as the longstanding political rationales that motivate Chinese global infrastructure are arguably still in place.

Economically, the BRI is aimed at serving a suite of national economic goals discussed in Section 2. Some of China's own domestic economic problems which have grown more acute in recent years – such as the lack of demand for domestic construction projects despite consistent investment stimulus by

---

[60] www.ft.com/content/9b2cb53f-e6f0-479e-bb94-a2e0c8680e88.
[61] www.yidaiyilu.gov.cn/xwzx/bwdt/308507.htm.

China's government – may provide continued emphasis on using overseas infrastructure to offload excess capacity and search for profitable investments.[62]

Politically, global infrastructure remains a distinct component of donor and lender toolkits for pursuing influence given its visibility and national presence. For the Chinese government in particular, both its long global infrastructure pedigree and more recent initiatives, such as the creation of the multilateral AIIB, have firmly entrenched infrastructure as China's perceived comparative advantage in global development – with reputational benefits and liabilities – relative to other major donors and lenders. It is unclear why the Chinese government would wish to relinquish this reputational cornerstone given its own conviction in the merits of infrastructure-led development and the influence potential of these projects, significant economic and political risks notwithstanding.

Moreover, Chinese global infrastructure is not a stranger to outside criticism, and some of its most major twentieth-century projects encountered elite and popular criticism within and outside host countries (e.g. Monson 2009, 148). The resilience of this project class despite external criticism and internal shifts in China's global development strategy suggests that global infrastructure will continue to feature prominently in China's development finance, even as the Chinese government has recently rhetorically eschewed "vanity projects" (面子工程) and advocated for "high-quality development" (高质量发展) activities along the BRI (Reuters Staff 2018; Xinhua 2021).

Escaping recency bias and viewing the BRI from a more wholistic perspective thus suggests that Chinese global infrastructure is here to stay. Initial outcomes of the recently concluded third Belt and Road Forum for International Cooperation, marking the 10th anniversary of the BRI, support this assertion. Xi Jinping's speech at the forum emphasized eight planned steps to support a high-quality BRI, and global infrastructure features prominently in several of them (Xinhua 2023). In the State Council's accompanying white paper, global infrastructures and infrastructure connectivity continue to feature as central pillars of China's approach (State Council 2023).

Of course, this is not to suggest that Chinese global infrastructure is static. The first decade of the BRI offered important lessons for China's government, which appears to have entered into a period of recalibration as it attempts to better grasp the economic and noneconomic risks of global infrastructure projects, including those related to influence externalities. One potential future outcome is a recalibrated BRI in which project planners from China and in host countries have stronger incentives to gather input from communities and domestic actors to

---

[62] It is also possible that additional policy goals, such as Renminbi internationalization, could serve as additional impetus for Chinese global infrastructure activity in the Global South.

achieve greater levels of pre-project buy-in by paying more attention to the socioeconomic and environmental costs created by high-profile infrastructure. A greater degree of infrastructure cofinancing by Chinese and non-Chinese official and commercial actors, including the AIIB and peer multilateral institutions, could also help improve project selection, financing, and implementation.

New forms of infrastructure are also increasingly appearing alongside "traditional" infrastructure. Digital and green projects appear set to occupy a greater space in the future of Chinese global infrastructure. The Digital Silk Road (DSR) was announced in 2015 and promotes international connectivity via digital infrastructure along the BRI. During a speech at the Belt and Road Forum in 2017, Xi Jinping promoted a "digital silk road" (数字丝绸之路) of connected technologies in the fields of digital economy, artificial intelligence, nanotechnology, and quantum computing (Xinhua 2017). Like China's physical global infrastructure, digital projects are motivated by an analogous combination of commercial and political factors (Triolo et al. 2020; Hillman 2021). At the same time, the DSR and digital infrastructures more generally have raised international concerns about exports of digital surveillance technology to developing countries (Greitens 2020).

During the same speech, Xi emphasized the importance of a second form of emerging global infrastructure: green, low-carbon, and sustainable development concepts. China's government has since continued to promote environmental sustainability along the BRI through a series of speeches, initiatives, and institutions. In a September 2021 speech addressed to the UNGA, Xi pledged that China would stop financing coal-fired power plants abroad. During the same speech, Xi introduced the "Global Development Initiative" (全球发展倡议) and emphasized the need for environmentally sustainable growth. In practice, evidence suggests that while China's government is taking steps to reduce the carbon footprint of BRI infrastructure, these efforts are highly uneven across host countries thus far (e.g. Harlan 2021).

In contrast, other major donors and creditors have not featured global infrastructure as centrally as China either rhetorically or in practice. Nor have they integrated their own development approaches with those of developing countries in the way that China's government has. Western development agencies drastically curtailed infrastructure investments in recent decades in hopes that the private sector would fill the infrastructure financing gap and because of concerns about corruption (e.g. Dollar 2008). Recent multilateral responses to the BRI, such as PGII or the Global Gateway, suggest that the reemergence of Chinese global infrastructure might galvanize these "traditional" donors and creditors to reverse course and significantly increase their provision of infrastructure to developing countries. But such initiatives face serious questions about scale and coordination, and it is unclear whether and the extent to which they will materialize (Lu and Myxter-lino 2021). If they do, these providers of development capital will also face complex economic and political consequences resulting from unexpected infrastructure trajectories, often involving mobilization and narratives, described earlier.

To summarize, Chinese global infrastructure is an older and more persistent phenomenon than popular accounts suggest. Historical and global context demonstrates that the BRI and contemporary Chinese global infrastructure are chapters in a larger story of infrastructure, development, and influence in world politics. In this vein, this Element also speaks to a new, broader agenda challenging "methodological nationalism" and the tendency to separate China from the world in analyzing its global connections (Franceschini and Loubere 2022, 37–38). Research that applies contexts and general concepts from other fields can improve our understanding of China's role in the world, and also potentially help refine these concepts themselves. For example, as argued in Section 4, evidence on Chinese global infrastructure suggests that earlier, straightforward approaches to studying China's influence were useful departure points but that more inclusive approaches may be needed to capture previously underappreciated, incidental influence processes that stem from infrastructure projects.

Future researchers can further refine and improve our understanding of the aims and effects of Chinese and other global infrastructures.[63] This Element defines Chinese global infrastructure and outlines two important project classes, high-profile and prestige projects. It exhaustively catalogues China's global infrastructure portfolio since 1949 and innovates on earlier datasets and research by directly collecting data on and measuring Chinese global infrastructure. Future studies can build on this initial progress by making use of the latest datasets, such as AidData's Global Chinese Development Finance Dataset, 3.0 (Custer et al. 2023), to track whether and how the composition of Chinese global infrastructure is shifting into digital and other forms. It also charts multiple inroads to China's infrastructure-influence nexus that could be more systematically unpacked. For instance, future research could more rigorously isolate and study the various influence pathways discussed earlier using a variety of approaches, from carefully designed survey experiments to in-country fieldwork. Finally, as digital global infrastructures become increasingly central components of China's global economic engagement, researchers can help further unpack how these projects generate similar or different influence processes than those outlined earlier.

---

[63] Future research could, for example, develop a systematic framework for evaluating the economic, political, and other returns of global infrastructure projects over longer periods of time. Researchers could also more rigorously comparatively assess the performance of Chinese global infrastructure relative to other infrastructure providers.

References

Alden, Chris. 2007. *China in Africa*. London: Zed Books.

Alden, Chris, and Cristina Alves. 2008. "History & Identity in the Construction of China's Africa Policy." *Review of African Political Economy* 35(115): 43–58.

Ali, Ifzal, and Ernesto M. Pernia. 2003. "Infrastructure and Poverty Reduction – What Is the Connection?" Asian Development Bank ERD Policy Brief Series Economics and Research Department No. 13.

Allan, Bentley, Srdjan Vucetic, and Ted Hopf. 2018. "The Distribution of Identity and the Future of International Order: China's Hegemonic Prospects." *International Organization* 72(4): 839–869.

Alkon, Meir, Xiaogang He, Aubrey R. Paris, et al. 2019. "Water Security Implications of Coal-fired Power Plants Financed through China's Belt and Road Initiative." *Energy Policy* 132: 1101–1109.

Altshuler, Alan A., and David E. Luberoff. 2004. *Mega-projects: The Changing Politics of Urban Public Investment*. Washington, DC.: Brookings Institution Press.

American Society of Civil Engineers. 2017. *Infrastructure Report Card: A Comprehensive Assessment of America's Infrastructure*. Reston: American Society of Civil Engineers.

Anand, Nikhil, Akhil Gupta, and Hannah Appel (eds.). 2018. *The Promise of Infrastructure*. Durham: Duke University Press.

Ansar, Atif, Bent Flyvbjerg, Alexander Budzier, and Daniel Lunn. 2016. "Does Infrastructure Investment Lead to Economic Growth or Economic Fragility? Evidence from China." *Oxford Review of Economic Policy* 32(3): 360–390.

Aschauer, David Alan. 1998. "Is Public Expenditure Productive?" *Journal of Monetary Economics* 23(2): 177–200.

Bader, Julia. 2015. "China, Autocratic Patron? An Empirical Investigation of China as a Factor in Autocratic Survival." *International Studies Quarterly* 59(1): 23–33.

Bai, Yu, Yanjun Li, and Yunuo Wang. 2022. "Chinese Aid and Local Political Attitudes." *Economic Modelling* 113: 105893.

Bailey, Michael A., Anton Strezhnev, and Erik Voeten. 2017. "Estimating Dynamic State Preferences from United Nations Voting Data." *Journal of Conflict Resolution* 61(2): 430–456.

Baldwin, Kate and Matthew S. Winters. 2020. "How Do Different Forms of Foreign Aid Affect Government Legitimacy? Evidence from an Informational

Experiment in Uganda." *Studies in Comparative International Development* 55(2): 160–183.

Banham, Reyner. 2020. *Megastructure: Urban Futures of the Recent Past.* New York: Monacelli Press.

Barbieri, Katherine, Omar Keshk and Brian Pollins. 2008. "Correlates of War Project Trade Data Set Codebook." Codebook Version 2.0 Mimeo.

Barnett, Michael and Raymond Duvall. 2005. "Power in International Politics." *International Organization* 59(1): 39–75.

Bartke, Wolfgang. 1989. *The Economic Aid of the PR China to Developing and Socialist Countries.* Munich: KG Saur Verlag Gmbh.

Baum-Snow, Nathaniel, Loren Brandt, J. Vernon Henderson, Matthew A. Turner, and Qinghua Zhang. 2017. "Roads, Railroads, and Decentralization of Chinese Cities." *Review of Economics and Statistics* 99(3): 435–448.

Benabdallah, Lina. 2021. "Spanning Thousands of Miles and Years: Political Nostalgia and China's Revival of the Silk Road." *International Studies Quarterly* 65(2): 294–305.

BenYishay, Ariel, Bradley Parks, Daniel Runfola, and Rachel Trichler. 2016. "Forest Cover Impacts of Chinese Development Projects in Ecologically Sensitive Areas." Williamsburg: AidData Working Paper No.32

Berman, Eli, Jacob N. Shapiro, and Joseph H. Felter. 2011. "Can Hearts and Minds Be Bought? The Economics of Counterinsurgency in Iraq." *Journal of Political Economy* 119(4): 766–819.

Bissio, Roberto. 2017. "Leveraging Corruption: How World Bank Funds Ended up Destabilizing Young Democracies in Latin America." In *Reclaiming Policies for the Public.* Civil Society Reflection Group on the 2030 Agenda for Sustainable Development: 154–156. www.2030spotlight.org/sites/default/files/download/spotlight_170626_final_web.pdf.

Bjørnskov, Christian, and Martin Rode. 2020. "Regime Types and Regime Change: A New Dataset on Democracy, Coups, and Political Institutions." *Review of International Organizations* 15(2): 531–551.

Blair, Robert A., Robert Marty, and Philip Roessler. 2022. "Foreign Aid and Soft Power: Great Power Competition in Africa in the Early Twenty-First Century." *British Journal of Political Science* 52(3): 1355–1376.

Bluhm, Richard, Axel Dreher, Andreas Fuchs, et al. 2021. "Connective Financing: Chinese Infrastructure Projects and the Diffusion of Economic Activity in Developing Countries." CESifo Working Paper No. 8344. Munich: Center for Economic Studies.

Bourdieu, Pierre. 1991. *Language and Symbolic Power.* Cambridge, MA: Harvard University Press.

Bräutigam, Deborah. 2009. *The Dragon's Gift: The Real Story of China in Africa*. Oxford: Oxford University Press.

Bräutigam, Deborah. 2011. "Aid 'with Chinese Characteristics': Chinese Foreign Aid and Development Finance Meet the OECD-DAC Aid Regime." *Journal of International Development* 23(5): 752–764.

Bräutigam, Deborah. 2019a. "Chinese Loans and African Structural Transformation." In Arkebe Oqubay and Justin Yifu Lin (eds.), *China–Africa and an Economic Transformation*. Oxford: Oxford University Press: 129–146.

Bräutigam, Deborah. 2019b. "Misdiagnosing the Chinese Infrastructure Push." *The American Interest*, April 4. www.the-american-interest.com/2019/04/04/misdiagnosing-the-chinese-infrastructure-push.

Bräutigam, Deborah. 2020. "A Critical Look at Chinese 'Debt-Trap Diplomacy': The Rise of a Meme." *Area Development and Policy* 5(1): 1–14.

Bräutigam, Deborah. 2023. "The Developing World's Coming Debt Crisis." *Foreign Affairs*. www.foreignaffairs.com/china/developing-worlds-coming-debt-crisis.

Bräutigam, Deborah, Vijay Bhalaki, Laure Deron, and Yinxuan Wang. 2022. "How Africa Borrows from China: And Why Mombasa Port Is Not Collateral for Kenya's Standard Gauge Railway." China–Africa Research Initiative Working Paper No. 52. Washington, DC: Johns Hopkins University School of Advanced International Studies.

Brazys, Samuel, and Alexander Dukalskis. 2019. "Rising Powers and Grassroots Image Management: Confucius Institutes and China in the Media." *The Chinese Journal of International Politics* 12(4): 557–584.

Brazys, Samuel, Johan A. Elkink, and Gina Kelly. 2017. "Bad Neighbors? How Co-located Chinese and World Bank Development Projects Impact Local Corruption in Tanzania." *Review of International Organizations* 12(2): 227–253.

Brazinsky, Gregg A. 2017. *Winning the Third World: Sino-American Rivalry during the Cold War*. Chapel Hill: University of North Carolina Press.

Breuer, Adam, and Alastair Iain Johnston. 2019. "Memes, Narratives and the Emergent US–China Security Dilemma." *Cambridge Review of International Affairs* 32(4): 429–455.

Briggs, Ryan C. 2012. "Electrifying the Base? Aid and Incumbent Advantage in Ghana." *The Journal of Modern African Studies* 50(4):603–624.

Bruner, Jerome S. 1990. *Acts of Meaning: Four Lectures on Mind and Culture* (Vol. 3). Cambridge: Harvard University Press.

Bueno De Mesquita, Bruce and Alastair Smith. 2007. "Foreign Aid and Policy Concessions," *Journal of Conflict Resolution* 51(2): 251–284.

Bueno De Mesquita, Bruce and Alastair Smith. 2009. "A Political Economy of Aid." *International Organization* 63(2): 309–340.

Bueno de Mesquita, Bruce, James D Morrow, Randolph M. Siverson, and Alastair Smith. 2003. *The Logic of Political Survival*. Cambridge, MA: MIT Press.

Bunkenborg, Mikkel, Morten Nielsen, and Morten Axel Pedersen. 2022. *Collaborative Damage: An Experimental Ethnography of Chinese Globalization*. Ithaca: Cornell University Press.

Burnside, Craig, and David Dollar. 2000. "Aid, Policies, and Growth." *American Economic Review* 90(4): 847–868.

Caixin. 2015. "习近平讲述'中国故事' 诠释官方外交语言新'温度' [Xi Jinping Tells 'China Stories,' Illustrating New 'Warmth' in Official Diplomatic Discourse]." 财新 [*Caixin*], April 23. www.caixin.com/2015–04-23/100802893.html.

Calderón, César, and Luis Servén. 2014. "Infrastructure, Growth, and Inequality: An Overview." World Bank Policy Research Working Paper No. 7034. Washington, D.C.: World Bank Group.

Camba, Alvin. 2020. "Derailing Development: China's Railway Projects and Financing Coalitions in Indonesia, Malaysia, and the Philippines." GCI Working Paper No. 008. Boston: Global Development Policy Center, Boston University. www.bu.edu/gdp/files/2020/02/WP8-Camba-Derailing-Development.pdf.

Camba, Alvin. 2021. "Sinews of Politics: State Grid Corporation, Investment Coalitions, and Embeddedness in the Philippines." *Energy Strategy Reviews* 35: 100640.

Carse, Ashley. 2016. "Keyword: Infrastructure–How a Humble French Engineering Term Shaped the Modern World." In Penelope Harvey, Casper Jensen, and Atsuro Morita, (eds.), *Infrastructures and Social Complexity: A Companion*. New York: Routledge: 45–57.

Centeno, Miguel Angel. 2002. *Blood and Debt: War and the Nation-state in Latin America*. University Park: Penn State Press.

Cha, Sujin, Yehzee Ryoo, and Sung Eun Kim. 2023. "Losing Hearts and Minds? Unpacking the Effects of Chinese Soft Power Initiatives in Africa." *Asian Survey* 63(1): 1–30.

Chan, Debby Sze Wan. 2017. "Asymmetric Bargaining between Myanmar and China in the Myitsone Dam Controversy: Social Opposition Akin to David's Stone against Goliath." *Pacific Review* 30(5): 674–691.

Chan, Debby Sze Wan. 2020. "China's Diplomatic Strategies in Response to Economic Disputes in Myanmar." *International Relations of the Asia-Pacific* 20(2): 307–336.

Cheibub, Jose Antonio, Jennifer Gandhi and James Raymond Vreeland. 2010. "Democracy and Dictatorship' Revisited." *Public Choice* 143(1–2): 67–101.

Chellaney, Brahma. 2017. "China's Debt-trap Diplomacy." *Project Syndicate* 23. www.project-syndicate.org/commentary/china-one-belt-one-road-loans-debt-by-brahma-chellaney-2017-01.

Chen, Muyang. 2020a. "Beyond Donation: China's Policy Banks and the Reshaping of Development Finance." *Studies in Comparative International Development* 55(4): 436–459.

Chen, Wanjing Kelly. 2020b. "Sovereign Debt in the Making: Financial Entanglements and Labor Politics along the Belt and Road in Laos." *Economic Geography* 96(4): 295–314.

Chen, Wanjing Kelly. 2022. "Harden the Hardline, Soften the Softline: Unravelling China's Qiaoling-centred Diaspora Governance in Laos." *China Quarterly* 250: 397–416.

Cheng, Joseph Y. S., and Huangao Shi. 2009. "China's African Policy in the Post-Cold War Era." *Journal of Contemporary Asia* 39(1): 87–115.

Cheng, Zhangxi and Ian Taylor. 2017. *China's Aid to Africa: Does Friendship Really Matter?* Oxford: Routledge.

Chin, Gregory T. 2012. "China as a 'Net Donor:' Tracking Dollars and Sense." *Cambridge Review of International Affairs* 25(4): 579–603.

CIA. 1982. Communist Aid to Non-Communist Less Developed Countries, 1981: A Reference Aid. Office of Global Issues. Available at https://www.cia.gov/readingroom/docs/DOC_0000497175.pdf.

Coppedge, Michael, John Gerring, Carl Henrik Knutsen, et al. 2020. "V-dem Dataset (v10)."

Corkin, Lucy. 2011. "Redefining Foreign Policy Impulses toward Africa: The Roles of the MFA, the MOFCOM and China Exim Bank." *Journal of Current Chinese Affairs* 40(4): 61–90.

Council on Foreign Relations. 2006. "The World Bank and Corruption." www.cfr.org/backgrounder/world-bank-and-corruption.

Cruz, Cesi and Christina J. Schneider. 2017. "Foreign Aid and Undeserved Credit Claiming." *American Journal of Political Science* 61(2): 396–408.

Custer, Samantha, Axel Dreher, Thai-Binh Elston, et al. 2021. *Tracking Chinese Development Finance: An Application of AidData's TUFF 2.0 Methodology.* Williamsburg: AidData at William & Mary.

Custer, Samantha, Axel Dreher, Thai-Binh Elston, et al. 2023. *Tracking Chinese Development Finance: An Application of AidData's TUFF 3.0 Methodology.* Williamsburg: AidData at William & Mary.

Custer, Samantha, Zachary Rice, Takaaki Masaki, Rebecca Latourell and Bradley Parks. 2015. *Listening to Leaders: Which Development Partners*

Do They Prefer and Why? Technical Report. Williamsburg: AidData at William & Mary.

Dahl, Robert. 1984. *Modern Political Analysis*. 4th ed. Englewood Cliffs: Prentice Hall.

de Goede, Marieke, and Carola Westermeier. 2022. "Infrastructural Geopolitics." *International Studies Quarterly* 66(3): sqac033

De Soyres, François, Alen Mulabdic, and Michele Ruta. 2020. "Common Transport Infrastructure: A Quantitative Model and Estimates from the Belt and Road Initiative." *Journal of Development Economics* 143: 102415.

DeHart, Monica. 2012. "Remodelling the Global Development Landscape: The China Model and South–South Cooperation in Latin America." *Third World Quarterly* 33(7): 1359–1375.

Denicke, Lars. 2011. "Fifty Years' Progress in Five: Brasilia – Modernization, Globalism, and the Geopolitics of Flight." In Gabrielle Hecht (ed.), *Entangled Geographies: Empire and Technopolitics in the Global Cold War*. Cambridge, MA: MIT Press: 185–186.

Dietrich, Simone, Minhaj Mahmud, and Matthew S. Winters. 2018. "Foreign Aid, Foreign Policy, and Domestic Government Legitimacy: Experimental Evidence from Bangladesh." *Journal of Politics* 80(1): 133–148.

Ding, Iza. 2020. "Performative Governance." *World Politics* 72(4):525–556.

Dollar, David. 2008. "Supply Meets Demand: Chinese Infrastructure Financing in Africa." World Bank Blog, July 10. Washington, DC: The World Bank. blogs. worldbank.org/eastasiapacific/supply-meets-demand-chinese-infrastructure-financing-in-africa.

Dittmer, Lowell. 1977. "Political Culture and Political Symbolism: Toward a Theoretical Synthesis." *World Politics* 29(4): 552–583.

Donaldson, Dave. 2018. "Railroads of the Raj: Estimating the Impact of Transportation Infrastructure." *American Economic Review* 108(4/5): 899–934.

Dornan, Matthew, and Philippa Brant. 2014. "Chinese Assistance in the Pacific: Agency, Effectiveness and the Role of Pacific Island Governments." *Asia and the Pacific Policy Studies* 1(2): 349–363.

Dourado, Leolino. 2023. "China-Backed Infrastructure in the Global South: Lessons from the Case of the Brazil–Peru Transcontinental Railway Project." *Third World Quarterly*, 44(4): 814–832.

Dreher, Axel, and Andreas Fuchs. 2015. "Rogue Aid? An Empirical Analysis of China's Aid Allocation." *Canadian Journal of Economics* 48(3): 988–1023.

Dreher, Axel, Andreas Fuchs, Brad Parks, Austin M. Strange, and Michael J. Tierney. 2018. "Apples and Dragon Fruits: The Determinants of Aid and Other Forms of State Financing from China to Africa." *International Studies Quarterly* 62(1): 182–194.

Dreher, Axel, Andreas Fuchs, Roland Hodler, et al. 2019. "African Leaders and the Geography of China's Foreign Assistance." *Journal of Development Economics* 140: 44–71.

Dreher, Axel, Andreas Fuchs, Bradley Parks, Austin Strange, and Michael J. Tierney. 2021. "Aid, China, and Growth: Evidence from a New Global Development Finance Dataset." *American Economic Journal: Economic Policy* 13(2): 135–174.

Dreher, Axel, Andreas Fuchs, Bradley Parks, Austin Strange, and Michael Tierney. 2022. *Banking on Beijing: The Aims and Impacts of China's Overseas Development Program*. Cambridge: Cambridge University Press.

Dreher, Axel, Jan-Egbert Sturm, and James Raymond Vreeland. 2009. "Development Aid and International Politics: Does Membership on the UN Security Council Influence World Bank Decisions?" *Journal of Development Economics* 88(1):1–18.

Duflo, Esther, and Rohini Pande. 2007. "Dams." *The Quarterly Journal of Economics* 122(2): 601–646.

Edelman, Murray Jacob. 1972. *The Symbolic Uses of Politics*. Urbana: University of Illinois Press.

Editorial Board. 2008. 方毅传 [*Biography of Fang Yi*]. Beijing: Renmin Chubanshe.

Eichenauer, Vera Z., Andreas Fuchs, and Lutz Brückner. 2021. "The Effects of Trade, Aid, and Investment on China's Image in Latin America." *Journal of Comparative Economics* 49(2): 483–498.

Eisenman, Joshua. 2018. "Comrades-in-Arms: The Chinese Communist Party's Relations with African Political Organisations in the Mao Era, 1949–76." *Cold War History* 18(4): 429–445.

Engerman, David C. 2018. *The Price of Aid: The Economic Cold War in India*. Cambridge, MA: Harvard University Press.

Esfahani, Hadi Salehi, and María Teresa Ramírez. 2003. "Institutions, Infrastructure, and Economic Growth." *Journal of Development Economics* 70(2): 443–477.

Estache, Antonio, and Marianne Fay. 2007. "Current Debates on Infrastructure Policy." Vol. 4410. World Bank.

Feenstra, Robert C., Robert Inklaar and Marcel P Timmer. 2015. "The Next Generation of the Penn World Table." *American Economic Review* 105(10): 3150–3182.

Fernald, John G. 1999. "Roads to Prosperity? Assessing the Link between Public Capital and Productivity." *American Economic Review* 89(3): 619–638.

Flores-Macias, Gustavo A., and Sarah E Kreps. 2013. "The Foreign Policy Consequences of Trade: China's Commercial Relations with Africa and Latin America, 1992–2006." *Journal of Politics* 75(02): 357–371.

Flyvbjerg, Bent (ed.). 2017. *The Oxford Handbook of Megaproject Management*. Oxford: Oxford University Press.

Flyvbjerg, Bent, Nils Bruzelius, and Werner Rothengatter. 2003. *Megaprojects and Risk: An Anatomy of Ambition*. Cambridge: Cambridge University Press.

Franceschini, Ivan, and Nicholas Loubere. 2022. *Global China as Method*. Cambridge: Cambridge University Press (Elements in Global China).

Frank, Robert H. 1985. *Choosing the Right Pond: Human Behavior and the Quest for Status*. Oxford: Oxford University Press.

Fredericks, Rosalind. 2018. *Garbarge Citizenship: Vital Infrastructures of Labor in Dakar, Senegal*. Durham: Duke University Press.

Fung, Courtney, Enze Han, Kai Quek, and Austin Strange. 2023. "Conditioning China's Influence: Intentionality, Intermediaries, and Institutions." *Journal of Contemporary China* 32(139): 1–16.

Gebreluel, Goitom. 2023. "Ideology, Grand Strategy and the Rise and Decline of Ethiopia's Regional Status." *International Affairs* 99(3): 1127–1147.

Gelpern, Anna, Sebastian Horn, Scott Morris, Brad Parks, and Christoph Trebesch. 2022. "How China Lends: A Rare Look into 100 Debt Contracts with Foreign Governments." *Economic Policy*: eiac054.

Ghossein, Tania, Bernard Hoekman, and Anirudh Shingal. 2018. "Public Procurement in the Belt and Road Initiative." World Bank MTI Global Pratice Discussion Paper No. 10.

Gibbons, Stephen, Teemu Lyytikäinen, Henry G. Overman, and Rosa Sanchis-Guarner. 2019. "New Road Infrastructure: The Effects on Firms." *Journal of Urban Economics* 110: 35–50.

Gill, Bates, and James Reilly. 2007. "The Tenuous Hold of China Inc. in Africa." *Washington Quarterly* 30(3): 37–52.

Goh, Evelyn. 2014. "The Modes of China's Influence: Cases from Southeast Asia." *Asian Survey* 54(5): 825–848.

Goldsmith, Benjamin E., and Yusaku Horiuchi. 2012. "In Search of Soft Power: Does Foreign Public Opinion Matter for US Foreign Policy?" *World Politics* 64(3): 555–585.

Goldsmith, Benjamin E., Yusaku Horiuchi, and Terence Wood. 2014. "Doing Well by Doing Good: The Impact of Foreign Aid on Foreign Public Opinion." *Quarterly Journal of Political Science* 9(1): 87–114.

Gowa, Joanne, and Edward D Mansfield. 1993. "Power Politics and International Trade." *American Political Science Review* 87(02): 408–420.

Greitens, Sheena Chestnut. 2020. "Dealing with Demand for China's Global Surveillance Exports." Brookings Institution Global China Report.

Guldi, Jo. 2012. *Roads to Power: Britain Invents the Infrastructure State.* Cambridge, MA: Harvard University Press.

Guo, Shiqi, and Haicheng Jiang. 2021. "Chinese Aid and Local Employment in Africa." Working Paper.

Hagström, Linus, and Karl Gustafsson. 2019. "Narrative Power: How Storytelling Shapes East Asian International Politics." *Cambridge Review of International Affairs* 32(4): 387–406.

Hameiri, Shahar, and Lee Jones. 2020. "Debunking the Myth of 'Debt-trap Diplomacy:' How Recipient Countries Shape China's Belt and Road Initiative." Research Paper. London: Chatham House. www.chathamhouse .org/sites/default/files/2020-08-19-debunking-myth-debt-trap-diplomacy-jones-hameiri.pdf.

Harding, Robin. 2015. "Attribution and Accountability: Voting for Roads in Ghana." *World Politics* 67(4): 656–689.

Harlan, Tyler. 2021. "Green Development or Greenwashing? A Political Ecology Perspective on China's Green Belt and Road." *Eurasian Geography and Economics* 62(2): 202–226.

Hawkins, Darren, Dan Nielson, Anna Bergevin, Ashley Hearn and Becky Perry. 2010. "Codebook for Assembling Data on China's Development Finance." Brigham Young University and College of William and Mary.

Herbst, Jeffrey. 2000. *States and Power in Africa: Comparative Lessons in Authority and Control.* Princeton: Princeton University Press.

Hillman, Jonathan E. 2019a. "Influence and Infrastructure: The Strategic Stakes of Foreign Projects." A Report of the CSIS Reconnecting Asia Project. Center for Strategic and International Studies. https://csis-website-prod.s3.amazonaws .com/s3fs-public/publication/190123_Hillman_InfluenceandInfrastructure_ WEB_v3.pdf.

Hillman, Jonathan E. 2019b. "Corruption Flows along China's Belt and Road." Center for Strategic and International Studies.

Hillman, Jonathan. 2020. *The Emperor's New Road: China and the Project of the Century.* New Haven: Yale University Press.

Hillman, Jonathan E. 2021. *The Digital Silk Road: China's Quest to Wire the World and Win the Future.* New York: HarperCollins.

Hirschman, Albert O. 1967. *Development Projects Observed.* Washington, DC.: Brookings Institution.

Ho, Selina. 2020. "Infrastructure and Chinese Power." *International Affairs* 96(6): 1461–1485.

Hodler, Roland, and Paul A. Raschky. 2014. "Regional Favoritism." *The Quarterly Journal of Economics* 129(2): 995–1033.

Horn, Sebastian, Bradley Parks, Carmen M. Reinhart, and Christoph Trebesch. 2023. "China as an International Lender of Last Resort." Working Paper No.124. Williamsburg: AidData at William & Mary.

Horvath, Janos. 1976. *Chinese Technology Transfer to the Third World: A Grants Economy Analysis*. New York: Praeger.

Huang, Zhengli, and Xiangming Chen. 2016. "Is China Building Africa?" *European Financial Review*, June 22. www.europeanfinancialreview.com/is-china-building-africa/.

Hughes, Alice C. 2019. "Understanding and Minimizing Environmental Impacts of the Belt and Road Initiative." *Conservation Biology* 33(4): 883–894.

Hurley, John, Scott Morris, and Gailyn Portelance. 2019. "Examining the Debt Implications of the Belt and Road Initiative from a Policy Perspective." *Journal of Infrastructure, Policy and Development* 3(1): 139–175.

Independent Evaluation Group. 2010. *Cost-Benefit Analysis in World Bank Projects*. Washington, DC: World Bank.

Independent Group of Scientists appointed by the Secretary-General. 2019. *Global Sustainable Development Report 2019: The Future Is Now – Science for Achieving Sustainable Development*. New York: United Nations.

Isaksson, Ann-Sofie, and Andreas Kotsadam. 2018. "Chinese Aid and Local Corruption." *Journal of Public Economics* 159: 146–159.

Ismael, Tareq Y. 1971. "The People's Republic of China and Africa." *The Journal of Modern African Studies* 9(4): 507–529.

Jones, Evan. 2021. "Winning Hearts and Minds or Stoking Resentment? Exploring the Effects of Chinese Foreign Aid on Africans' Perceptions of China." Working Paper.

Kao, Michael Y. M. 1988. "Taiwan's and Beijing's Campaigns for Unification," In Harvey Feldman, Michael Y. M. Kao and Ilpyong J. Kim (eds.), *Taiwan in a Time of Transition*. New York: Paragon House: 175–200.

Kaplan, Stephen B. 2021. *Globalizing Patient Capital: The Political Economy of Chinese Finance in the Americas*. Cambridge: Cambridge University Press.

Kardon, Isaac B., and Wendy Leutert. 2022. "Pier Competitor: China's Power Position in Global Ports." *International Security* 46(4): 9–47.

Kastner, Scott L. 2016. "Buying Influence? Assessing the Political Effects of China's International Trade." *Journal of Conflict Resolution* 60(6): 980–1007.

Kastner, Scott L., and Margaret M. Pearson. 2021. "Exploring the Parameters of China's Economic Influence." *Studies in Comparative International Development* 56(1): 18–44.

Kazantsev, Andrei, Svetlana Medvedeva, and Ivan Safranchuk. 2021. "Between Russia and China: Central Asia in Greater Eurasia." *Journal of Eurasian Studies* 12(1): 57–71.

Ker, Michelle. 2017. "China's High-speed Rail Diplomacy." US-China Economic and Security Review Commission.

Khalili, Laleh. 2021. *Growing Pains*. London Review of Books 43(6).

Kim, Hyo-Sook. 2018. "The Political Drivers of South Korea's Official Development Assistance to Myanmar." *Contemporary Southeast Asia* 40(3): 475–502.

Kinney, Sasha. 2022. "Lamu Coal Power Plant," The People's Map of Global China, January 22. https://thepeoplesmap.net/project/lamu-coal-power-plant/.

Kobayashi, Takaaki. 2008. "Evolution of China's Aid Policy." JBICI Working Paper No. 27. Tokyo: Japan Bank for International Cooperation. www.jica.go.jp/jica-ri/IFIC_and_JBICI-Studies/jica-ri/english/publication/archives/jbic/report/working/pdf/wp27_e.pdf.

Kong, Bo, and Kevin P. Gallagher. 2017. "Globalizing Chinese Energy Finance: The Role of Policy Banks." *Journal of Contemporary China* 26(108): 834–851.

Krebs, Ronald R. 2015. *Narrative and the Making of US National Security*. Cambridge: Cambridge University Press.

Kuik, Cheng-Chwee. 2021. "Elite Legitimation and the Agency of the Host Country." In Florian Schneider (ed.), *Global Perspectives on China's Belt and Road Initiative*. Amsterdam: Amsterdam University Press: 217–244.

Kuziemko, Ilyana, and Eric Werker. 2006. "How Much Is a Seat on the Security Council Worth? Foreign Aid and Bribery at the United Nations." *Journal of Political Economy* 114(5): 905–930.

Lampton, David M., Selina Ho, and Cheng-Chwee Kuik. 2020. *Rivers of Iron: Railroads and Chinese Power in Southeast Asia*. Berkeley: University of California Press.

Large, Daniel. 2008. "Beyond 'Dragon in the Bush': The Study of China–Africa Relations." *African Affairs* 107(426): 45–61.

Larkin, Brian. 2013. "The Politics and Poetics of Infrastructure." *Annual Review of Anthropology* 42: 327–343.

Larkin, Brian. 2018. "Promising Forms: The Political Aesthetics of Infrastructure." In Nikhil Anand, Akhil Gupta, and Hannah Appel (eds.), *The Promise of Infrastructure*. Durham: Duke University Press: 175–202.

Latham, Michael E. 2011. *The Right Kind of Revolution: Modernization, Development, and U.S. Foreign Policy from the Cold War to the Present.* Ithaca: Cornell University Press.

Law, Yu Fai. 1984. *Chinese Foreign Aid: A Study of Its Nature and Goals with Particular Reference to the Foreign Policy and World View of the People's Republic of China, 1950–1982.* Fort Lauderdale: Breitenbach.

Leduc, Sylvain, and Daniel Wilson. 2013. "Roads to Prosperity or Bridges to Nowhere? Theory and Evidence on the Impact of Public Infrastructure Investment." *NBER Macroeconomics Annual* 27(1): 89–142.

Lee, Ching Kwan. 2017. *The Specter of Global China: Politics, Labor, and Foreign Investment in Africa.* Chicago: University of Chicago Press.

Lei, Zhenhuan, and Junlong Aaron Zhou. 2022. "Private Returns to Public Investment: Political Career Incentives and Infrastructure Investment in China." *Journal of Politics* 84(1): 455–469.

Lekorwe, Mogopodi, Anyway Chingwete, Mina Okuru and Romaric Samson. 2016. "China's Growing Presence in Africa Wins Largely Positive Popular Reviews." Afrobarometer Dispatch No. 122.

Leslie, Agnes Ngoma. 2016. "Zambia and China: Workers' Protest, Civil Society and the Role of Opposition Politics in Elevating State Engagement." *African Studies Quarterly* 16(3): 89–106.

Leutert, Wendy. 2019. The Overseas Expansion and Evolution of Chinese State-Owned Enterprises. Fairbank Center Blog. July 11; https://medium.com/fairbank-center/the-overseas-expansion-and-evolution-of-chinese-state-owned-enterprises-3dc04134c5f2.

Li, Tania Murray. 2007. *The Will to Improve: Governmentality, Development, and the Practice of Politics.* Durham: Duke University Press.

Lim, Guanie. 2014. "The Internationalisation of Mainland Chinese Firms into Malaysia: From Obligated Embeddedness to Active Embeddedness." *Journal of Current Southeast Asian Affairs* 33(2): 59–90.

Lim, Guanie, Chen Li, and Xianbai Ji. 2022. "Chinese Financial Statecraft in Southeast Asia: An Analysis of China's Infrastructure Provision in Malaysia." *Pacific Review* 35(4): 647–675.

Lin, Justin Yifu, and Yan Wang. 2017. *Going beyond Aid: Development Cooperation for Structural Transformation.* Cambridge: Cambridge University Press.

Lin, Teh-chang. 1993. *The Foreign Aid Policy of the People's Republic of China: A Theoretical Analysis.* Doctoral Dissertation. Northern Illinois University. www.proquest.com/openview/eff07bf850e24c577e7ebf6e55c674ec/1?pq-origsite=gscholar&cbl=18750&diss=y.

Liu, Hong and Guanie Lim. 2019. "The Political Economy of a Rising China in Southeast Asia: Malaysia's Response to the Belt and Road Initiative." *Journal of Contemporary China* 28(116): 216–231.

Lorenzini, Sara. 2019. *Global Development: A Cold War History*. Princeton: Princeton University Press.

Lu, Juliet and Erik Myxter-lino. 2021. "Beyond Competition: Why the BRI and the B3W Can't and Shouldn't Be Considered Rivals." Rosa Luxemburg Stiftung. rosalux.nyc/belt-and-road-initiative-build-back-better-world.

Lukes, Steven. 2005. *Power: A Radical View*. 2nd ed. Basingstoke: Palgrave Macmillan.

Ma, Damien. 2011. "China's Long, Bumpy Road to High-Speed Rail." *The Altantic*. March 30.

Ma, Xiao. 2022. *Localized Bargaining: The Political Economy of China's High-Speed Railway Program*. Oxford: Oxford University Press.

Maçães, Bruno. 2018. *Belt and Road: A Chinese World Order*. London: Hurst.

Maizels, Alfred, and Machiko K Nissanke. 1984. "Motivations for Aid to Developing Countries." *World Development* 12(9):879–900.

Malik, Ammar A., Bradley Parks, Brooke Russell, et al. 2021. *Banking on the Belt and Road: Insights from a New Global Dataset of 13,427 Chinese Development Projects*. Williamsburg: AidData at William & Mary.

Mani, Anandi, and Sharun Mukand. 2007. "Democracy, Visibility and Public Good Provision." *Journal of Development Economics* 83(2): 506–529.

Mann, Michael. 1984. "The Autonomous Power of the State: Its Origins, Mechanisms and Results." *European Journal of Sociology/Archives Européennes de Sociologie* 25(2): 185–213.

Marchesi, Silvia, Tania Masi, and Saumik Paul. 2021. "Project Aid and Firm Performance." University of Milan Bicocca Department of Economics, Management and Statistics Working Paper No. 479.

Marshall, Monty G., and Keith Jaggers. 2002. *Polity IV Project: Political Regime Characteristics and Transitions, 1800–2002. Dataset User's Manual*. College Park: University of Maryland.

Marx, Benjamin. 2018. "Elections as Incentives: Project Completion and Visibility in African Politics." Working Paper. https://drive.google.com/file/d/1aSDEhq-ZGlUcX5QxWbb-0bAcAdSUXlKc/view.

Mawdsley, Emma. 2012. "The Changing Geographies of Foreign Aid and Development Cooperation: Contributions from Gift Theory." *Transactions of the Institute of British Geographers* 37(2): 256–272.

Mayer, T., and S Zignago. 2011. "Notes on CEPII's Distances Measures: The Geodist Database." Paris: CEPII Working Paper No. 201125, Centre d'Etudes Prospectives et d'Informations Internationales.

McCauley, John F., Margaret M. Pearson, and Xiaonan Wang. 2022. "Does Chinese FDI in Africa Inspire Support for a China Model of Development?" *World Development* 150: 105738.

McKinsey Global Institute. 2016. *Bridging Global Infrastructure Gaps*.

Meernik, James, Eric L. Krueger, and Steven C. Poe. 1998. "Testing Models of US Foreign Policy: Foreign Aid during and after the Cold War." *Journal of Politics* 60(1): 63–85.

Menga, Filippo. 2015. "Building a Nation through a Dam: The Case of Rogun in Tajikistan." *Nationalities Papers* 43(3):479–494.

Merrow, Edward W. 2011. *Industrial Megaprojects: Concepts, Strategies, and Practices for Success*. Hoboken: John Wiley.

Mertha, Andrew. 2014. *Brothers in Arms: Chinese Aid to the Khmer Rouge, 1975–1979*. Ithaca: Cornell University Press.

Meservey, Joshua. 2020. "Government Buildings in Africa Are a Likely Vector for Chinese Spying." Washington, DC: The Heritage Foundation Backgrounder No. 3476.

Mingey, Matthew, and Agatha Kratz. 2021. China's Belt and Road: Down But Not Out. Rhodium Group. https://rhg.com/research/bri-down-out/.

Monson, Jamie. 2009. *Africa's Freedom Railway: How a Chinese Development Project Changed Lives and Livelihoods in Tanzania*. Bloomington: Indiana University Press.

Monson, Jamie. 2021. "Learning by Heart: Training for Self-Reliance on the TAZARA Railway, 1968–1976." *Made in China Journal* 6(2): 95–103.

Moore, W. Gyude. 2018. "The Case against Branding Development Aid in Fragile States." Center for Global Development. www.cgdev.org/blog/case-against-branding-development-aidfragile-states.

Morgan, Pippa. 2019. "Can China's Economic Statecraft Win Soft Power in Africa? Unpacking Trade, Investment and Aid." *Journal of Chinese Political Science* 24(3): 387–409.

Morgan, Pippa, and Yu Zheng. 2019. "Tracing the Legacy: China's Historical Aid and Contemporary Investment in Africa." *International Studies Quarterly* 63(3): 558–573.

Moyo, Dambisa. 2009. Dead Aid: Why Aid Is Not Working and How There Is a Better Way for Africa. New York: Farrar, Straus and Giroux.

Mueller, Joris. 2022. "China's Foreign Aid: Political Determinants and Economic Effects." Working Paper. www.jorismueller.com/files/chinaaid_latest_draft.pdf.

Müller-Mahn, Detlef, Kennedy Mkutu, and Eric Kioko. 2021. "Megaprojects – Mega Failures? The Politics of Aspiration and the Transformation of Rural Kenya." *European Journal of Development Research* 33(4): 1069–1090.

Naim, Moises. 2007. "Rogue Aid." *Foreign Policy* 159 (March/April): 95–96.

Norris, William J. 2016. *Chinese Economic Statecraft: Commercial Actors, Grand Strategy, and State Control.* Ithaca: Cornell University Press.

Nye, Joseph S. 2004. *Soft Power: The Means to Success in World Politics.* New York: Public Affairs.

Nyíri, Pál, and Danielle Tan, eds. 2017. *Chinese Encounters in Southeast Asia: How People, Money, and Ideas from China are Changing a Region.* Seattle: University of Washington Press.

OECD. 1978. *The Aid Programme of China.* Paris: Organisation for Economic Cooperation and Development.

O'Neill, Barry. 2001. *Honor, Symbols, and War.* Ann Arbor: University of Michigan Press.

OFDA/CRED. 2018. *EM-DAT: the OFDA/CRED International Disasters Database.* Center forResearch on the Epidemiology of Disasters (CRED).

Office of the Secretary of State. 2020. *The Elements of the China Challenge.* Washington, DC: The Policy Planning Staff. www.state.gov/wpcontent/uploads/2020/11/20-02832-Elements-of-China-Challenge-508.pdf.

Oh, Yoon Ah. 2018. "Power Asymmetry and Threat Points: Negotiating China's Infrastructure Development in Southeast Asia." *Review of International Political Economy* 25(4): 530–552.

Owen IV, John M. 2010. *The Clash of Ideas in World Politics: Transnational Networks, States, and Regime Change, 1510–2010.* Princeton: Princeton University Press.

Oya, Carlos, and Florian Schaefer. 2023. "Do Chinese Firms in Africa Pay Lower Wages? A Comparative Analysis of Manufacturing and Construction Firms in Angola and Ethiopia." *World Development* 168: 106266. www.sciencedirect.com/science/article/pii/S0305750X23000840#:~:text=We%20analyse%20wage%20differences%20between,pay%20less%20than%20comparable%20firms.

Patey, Luke. 2021. *How China Loses: The Pushback against Chinese Global Ambitions.* New York: Oxford University Press.

Patterson, Molly, and Kristen Renwick Monroe. 1998. "Narrative in Political Science." *Annual Review of Political Science* 1(1): 315–331.

Pence, Mike. 2018. "Remarks by Vice President Pence on the Administration's Policy toward China." Washington, DC: The Hudson Institute, October 4.

People's Daily. 2022. "高质量共建'一带一路'成绩斐然 [Remarkable Achievement of High-quality Joint Construction of the 'Belt and Road Initiative']. *People's Daily.* January 25. www.gov.cn/xinwen/2022-01/25/content_5670280.htm.

Pettis, Michael. 2022. "The Only Five Paths China's Economy Can Follow." Carnegie Endowment for International Peace China Financial Markets. Available at https://carnegieendowment.org/chinafinancialmarkets/87007.

Ping, Szu-Ning, Yi-Ting Wang, and Wen-Yang Chang. 2022. "The Effects of China's Development Projects on Political Accountability." *British Journal of Political Science* 52(1): 65–84.

Ratigan, Kerry. 2021. "Are Peruvians Enticed by the 'China Model?' Chinese Investment and Public Opinion in Peru." *Studies in Comparative International Development* 56(1): 87–111.

Ray, Rebecca. 2023. "'Small Is Beautiful': A New Era in China's Overseas Development Finance?" Boston University Global Development Policy Center GCI Policy Brief 17.

Ren, Xuefei. 2017. "Biggest Infrastructure Bubble Ever?" In Bent Flyvbjerg (ed.), *The Oxford Handbook of Megaproject Management*. Oxford: Oxford University Press: 137–151.

Reuters Staff. 2018. "China's Xi Says Funds for Africa Not for 'Vanity Projects'." *Reuters*. September 3. www.reuters.com/article/china-africa-idUSL3N1VO018.

Rich, Timothy S. 2009. "Status for Sale: Taiwan and the Competition for Diplomatic Recognition." *Issues & Studies* 45(4): 159–188.

Rinck, Patricia. 2019. "'We Are Black Chinese' – Making Sense of APC's Pro-China Campaign in Sierra Leone's 2018 Elections." In Christof Hartmann and Nele Noesselt (eds.), *China's New Role in African Politics from Non-Intervention towards Stabilization?* London: Routledge: 213–228.

Roberts, Mark, Uwe Deichmann, Bernard Fingleton, and Tuo Shi. 2012. "Evaluating China's Road to Prosperity: A New Economic Geography Approach." *Regional Science and Urban Economics* 42(4): 580–594.

Robinson, James A. and Ragnar Torvik. 2005. "White Elephants." *Journal of Public Economics* 89(2–3): 197–210.

Rolland, Nadège. 2017. "China's 'Belt and Road Initiative': Underwhelming or game-changer?" *The Washington Quarterly* 40(1): 127–142.

Roller, Lars-Hendrik, and Leonard Waverman. 2001. "Telecommunications Infrastructure and Economic Development: A Simultaneous Approach." *American Economic Review* 91(4): 909–923.

Rotberg, Robert I. (ed.). 2009. *China into Africa: Trade, Aid, and Influence*. Washington, DC: Brookings Institution Press.

Rowley, Anthony H. 2020. *Foundations of the Future: The Global Battle for Infrastructure*. Singapore: World Scientific Publishing.

Rudyak, Marina. 2019a. "The Ins and Outs of China's International Development Agency." Beijing: Carnegie-Tsinghua Center for Global Policy.

Rudyak, Marina. 2019b. "CIDCA Issues Draft of 'Measures for the Use of Foreign Aid Logo'." China Aid Blog. http://china-aid-blog.com/2019/11/04/cidca-issues-draft-of-measures-for-theuse-of-chinese-aid-logo/.

Russel, Daniel R., and Blake H. Berger. 2020. *Weaponizing the Belt and Road Initiative*. New York: Asia Society Policy Institute Report.

Sajjad, Fizzah, and Umair Javed. 2022. "Democracy, Legitimacy, and Mega-Project Politics: The Evolution of Lahore's First BRT Corridor." *Antipode* 54(5): 1497–1518.

Sanchez-Robles, Blanca. 1998. "Infrastructure Investment and Growth: Some Empirical Evidence." *Contemporary Economic Policy* 16(1): 98–108.

Sanderson, Henry, and Michael Forsythe. 2013. *China's Superbank: Debt, Oil and Influence- How China Development Bank Is Rewriting the Rules of Finance*. Singapore: John Wiley.

Sauer, Jürgen MT, Laura Díaz Anadón, Julian Kirchherr, Judith Plummer Braeckman, and Vera Schulhof. 2022. "Determinants of Chinese and Western-backed Development Finance in the Global Electricity Sector." *Joule* 6(6): 1230–1252.

Schatz, Edward. 2021. *Slow Anti-Americanism: Social Movements and Symbolic Politics in Central Asia*. Palo Alto: Stanford University Press.

Scott, James C. 1998. *Seeing Like a State: How Certain Schemes to Improve the Human Condition Have Failed*. New Haven: Yale University Press.

Searsey, Dionne. 2015. "Poor in Guinea, but Making a Living From Crisp New Banknotes." *New York Times*. October 8, 2018. www.nytimes.com/2015/12/04/world/africa/guineaconakry-currency.html.

Sheridan, Derek. 2022. "'We Are Now the Same:' Chinese Wholesalers and the Politics of Trade Hierarchies in Tanzania." *China Quarterly* 250: 376–396.

Shi, Lin [石林主编]. 1989. Contemporary China: Economic Cooperation with Foreign Countries [当代中国的对外经济合作]. 北京: 中国社会科学出版社.

Shi, Weiyi. 2015. "The Political Economy of China's Outward Direct Investments." Ph.D. Dissertation, University of California San Diego.

Shikwati, James, Nashon Adero, and Josephat Juma. 2022. "The Clash of Systems: African Perceptions of the European Union and China Engagement." Friedrich Naumann Foundation for Freedom Working Paper.

Siu, Helen F., and Mike McGovern. 2017. "China–Africa Encounters: Historical Legacies and Contemporary Realities." *Annual Review of Anthropology* 46: 337–355.

Smith, Alastair. 2008. "The Perils of Unearned Income." *Journal of Politics* 70(3): 780–793.

Star, Susan Leigh. 1999. "The Ethnography of Infrastructure." *American Behavioral Scientist* 43(3): 377–391.

State Council. 2013. "Guidelines to Resolve Serious Overcapacity Problems. State Decree No. 41." Central People's Government of the People's Republic of China, October 15. www.gov.cn/zwgk/2013–10/15/content_2507143.htm.

State Council. 2021. "Full Text: China's International Development Cooperation in the New Era." Beijing: State Council Information Office. http://english.scio.gov.cn/whitepapers/2021-01/10/content_77099782.htm.

State Council. 2023. "The Belt and Road Initiative: A Key Pillar of the Global Community of Shared Future." Beijing: State Council Information Office. http://www.scio.gov.cn/zfbps/zfbps_2279/202310/t20231010_773734.html.

Steinberg, Gerald M. 1987. "Large-scale National Projects as Political Symbols: The Case of Israel." *Comparative Politics* 19(3):331–346.

Strange, Austin. 2023a. "Infrastructure and Incumbency: Evidence from Chinese Development Finance since 1949." Working Paper.

Strange, Austin. 2023b. "Symbols of State: Explaining Prestige Projects in the Global South." Working Paper.

Strange, Austin. Forthcoming. "Influence and Support for Foreign Aid: Evidence from the United States and China." *Review of International Organizations.*

Strange, Austin M., Axel Dreher, Andreas Fuchs, Bradley Parks, and Michael J. Tierney. 2017. "Tracking Underreported Financial Flows: China's Development Finance and the Aid–conflict Nexus Revisited." *Journal of Conflict Resolution* 61(5): 935–963.

Strange, Austin, Bradley Parks, Michael J. Tierney, et al. 2013. "China's Development Finance to Africa: A Media-based Approach to Data Collection." Center for Global Development Working Paper No. 323. Washington, D.C.

Strange, Austin, Elizabeth Plantan, and Wendy Leutert. 2023. "Complementary Partners? Attitudes toward Multi-Actor Development Projects in the Democratic Republic of Congo." Working Paper.

Sun, Irene Yuan, Kartik Jayaram, and Omid Kassiri. 2017. *Dance of the Lions and Dragons: How Are Africa and China Engaging, and How will the Partnership Evolve?* Mckinsey.www.mckinsey.com/~/media/mckinsey/fea tured%20insights/middle%20east%20and%20africa/the%20closest% 20look%20yet%20at%20chinese%20economic%20engagement%20in% 20africa/dance-of-the-lions-and-dragons.ashx.

Swedlund, Haley J. 2017. "Is China Eroding the Bargaining Power of Traditional Donors in Africa?" *International Affairs* 93(2): 389–408.

Tang, Xiaoyang. 2021. *Coevolutionary Pragmatism: Approaches and Impacts of China-Africa Economic Cooperation.* Cambridge: Cambridge University Press.

Terrefe, Biruk. 2020. "Urban Layers of Political Rupture: The 'New' Politics of Addis Ababa's Megaprojects." *Journal of Eastern African Studies* 14(3): 375–395.

The Economist 2017. "China Goes to Africa." *The Economist*. July 22.

Tilly, Charles. 1990. *Coercion, Capital, and European states, AD 990–1992.* Malden: Wiley-Blackwell.

Triolo, Paul, Kevin Allison, Clarise Brown, and Kelsey Broderick. 2020. "The Digital Silk Road: Expanding China's Digital Footprint." Eurasia Group.

Tritto, Angela. 2020. "Contentious Embeddedness: Chinese State Capital and the Belt and Road Initiative in Indonesia." *Made in China Journal* 5(1): 182–187.

Trump, Donald J. 2017. *National Security Strategy of the United States of America.* Executive Office of The President Washington, DC.

Tull, Denis M. 2006. "China's Engagement in Africa: Scope, Significance and Consequences." *Journal of Modern African Studies* 44(3): 459–479.

Umarov, Temur. 2021. "Dangerous Liaisons: How China Is Taming Central Asia's Elites." Carnegie Moscow Center. January 29. https://carnegie.ru/commentary/83756.

van der Westhuizen, Janis. 2007. "Glitz, Glamour and the Gautrain: Mega-Projects as Political Symbols." *Politikon* 34(3): 333–351.

Verri, Valeria Guzmán. 2020. "Gifting Architecture: China and the National Stadium in Costa Rica, 2007–11." *Architectural History* 63: 283–311.

Wade, Abdoulaye. 2008. "Time for the West to Practise What It Preaches." *Financial Times*. January 24. www.ft.com/content/5d347f88-c897-11dc-94a6-0000779fd2ac.

Wade, Robert H. 2016. "Boulevard to Broken Dreams, Part 1: The Polonoroeste Road Project in the Brazilian Amazon, and the World Bank's Environmental and Indigenous Peoples' Norms." *Brazilian Journal of Political Economy* 36: 214–230.

Wahba, Sadek. 2021. *Integrating Infrastructure in US Domestic and Foreign Policy.* Washington, DC: Wilson Center.

Wang, Lin. 2017. "林毅夫: 中国推动"一带一路"基建的四个比较优势"[Lin Yifu: China's Four Comparative Advantages in Promoting 'Belt and Road Initiative' Infrastructure Construction]. 第一财经. November 30 . https://m.yicai.com/news/5379021.html.

Wang, Yuan. 2022. "Executive Agency and State Capacity in Development: Comparing Sino-African Railways in Kenya and Ethiopia." *Comparative Politics* 54(2): 349–377.

Warmerdam, Ward, and Meine Pieter van Dijk. 2013. "Chinese State-Owned Enterprise Investments in Uganda: Findings from a Recent Survey of

Chinese Firms in Kampala." *Journal of Chinese Political Science* 18(3): 281–301.

Warner, Andrew M., Andrew Berg, and Catherine A Pattillo. 2014. "Public Investment as an Engine of Growth." Washington, DC: International Monetary Fund.

Wedeen, Lisa. 2015. *Ambiguities of Domination: Domination: Politics, Rhetoric and Symbols in Contemporary Syria*. Chicago: University of Chicago Press.

Weghorst, Keith R and Staffan I Lindberg. 2013. "What Drives the Swing Voter in Africa?" *American Journal of Political Science* 57(3):717–734.

Wellner, Lukas, Axel Dreher, Andreas Fuchs, Brad Parks, and Austin Strange. Forthcoming. "Can Aid Buy Foreign Public Support? Evidence from Chinese Development Finance." *Economic Development and Cultural Change*.

Wells, Louis T., and Eric S. Gleason. 1995. "Is Foreign Infrastructure Investment Still Risky?" *Harvard Business Review* 73(5): 44–53.

Westad, Odd Arne. 2005. *The Global Cold War: Third World Interventions and the Making of Our Times*. Cambridge: Cambridge University Press.

Williams, Martin J. 2017. "The Political Economy of Unfinished Development Projects: Corruption, Clientelism, or Collective Choice?" *American Political Science Review* 111(4): 705–723.

Winters, Matthew S. 2014. "Targeting, Accountability and Capture in Development Projects." *International Studies Quarterly* 58(2): 393–404.

Winters, Matthew S. 2019. "Too Many Cooks in the Kitchen? The Division of Financing in World Bank Projects and Project Performance." *Politics and Governance* 7(2): 117–126.

Wong, Audrye. 2021. "How Not to Win Allies and Influence Geopolitics: China's Self-Defeating Economic Statecraft." *Foreign Affairs* 100: 44–53.

Woods, Ngaire. 2008. "Whose Aid? Whose Influence? China, Emerging Donors and the Silent Revolution in Development Assistance." *International Affairs* 84(6): 1205–1221.

World Bank. 1994. *World Development Report 1994: Infrastructure for Development*. Washington, DC: World Bank.

World Bank. 2017. *World Development Indicators 2017*. Washington, DC: World Bank.

Xi, Jinping. 2021. "习近平出席第三次"一带一路"建设座谈会并发表重要讲话" [Xi Jinping Attends and Delivers Important Speech at Third High-Level Symposium on the Construction of the 'Belt and Road Initiative'], Xinhua News Agency, November 19. www.gov.cn/xinwen/2021-11/19/con tent_5652067.htm.

Xinhua. 2017. "Full Text of President Xi's Speech at Opening of Belt and Road Forum." May 14. www.xinhuanet.com//english/2017-05/14/c_136282982.htm.

Xinhua. 2021. '坚定不移推动共建"一带一路"高质量发展—习近平总书记在第三次"一带一路"建设座谈会上的重要讲话引发与会人员热烈反响 [Resolutely Promoting the Co-Construction of "Belt and Road" High-Quality Development—Important Speech by General Secretary Xi Jinping in the Third "Belt and Road" Conference Stimulates Enthusiastic Responses]. Chinese Government Website, November 20. www.gov.cn/xinwen/2021-11/20/content_5652108.htm.

Xinhua. 2023. "Full text of Xi Jinping's keynote speech at 3rd Belt and Road Forum for Int'l Cooperation" October 18. https://english.news.cn/20231018/7bfc16ac51d443c6a7a00ce25c972104/c.html.

Xu, Zhicheng Phil, and Yu Zhang. 2020. "Can Chinese Aid Win the Hearts and Minds of Africa's Local Population?" *Economic Modelling* 90: 322–330.

Yang, Hongbo, B. Alexander Simmons, Rebecca Ray, et al. 2021. "Risks to Global Biodiversity and Indigenous Lands from China's Overseas Development Finance." *Nature Ecology & Evolution* 5(11): 1520–1529.

Ye, Min. 2020. *The Belt Road and Beyond: State-Mobilized Globalization in China: 1998–2018.* Cambridge: Cambridge University Press.

Yeh, Emily T., and Elizabeth Wharton. 2016. "Going West and Going Out: Discourses, Migrants, and Models in Chinese Development." *Eurasian Geography and Economics* 57(3): 286–315.

Yu, George T. 1977. "China's Role in Africa." *Annals of the American Academy of Political and Social Science* 432(1): 96–109.

Zeitz, Alexandra O. 2021. "Emulate or Differentiate? Chinese Development Finance, Competition, and World Bank Infrastructure Funding." *The Review of International Organizations* 16(2): 265–292.

Zhang, Hong. 2020. "The Aid–Contracting Nexus: The Role of the International Contracting Industry in China's Overseas Development Engagements." *China Perspectives* 4: 17–27.

Zhang, Hong. 2023. "From Contractors to Investors? Evolving Engagement of Chinese State Capital in Global Infrastructure Development and the Case of Lekki Port in Nigeria. SAIS-CARI Working Paper No. 2023/53.

Zhang, Denghua, and Graeme Smith. 2017. "China's Foreign Aid System: Structure, Agencies, and Identities." *Third World Quarterly* 38(10): 2330–2346.

Zhao, Jianzhi, and Yijia Jing. 2019. "The Governance of China's Foreign Aid System: Evolution and Path Dependence." *Public Administration and Development* 39(4–5): 182–192.

Zhou, Hong, and Hou Xiong (eds.). 2017. *China's Foreign Aid: 60 Years in Retrospect.* Singapore: Springer.

Acknowledgments

The University of Hong Kong, the Hong Kong Research Grants Council (#27602621), and the Wilson Center provided generous research support for this Element. James Bedford, Tsz Him Chan, Hoi Ying Cheng, Ziqi Ding, Songtao Duan, Yu Han, Boyung Kim, Wing Hei Lam, Tsz Shan Lau, Dongxiao Li, Jiali Luo, Ho Yin Ma, Dilang Mo, Guanzheng Sun, Oi Ling Szeto, Yue Tang, Shihan Wang, Amy Wu, Yanyan Wu, Hanxiong Yan, Aozuo Zheng, Haoning Zheng, and Xinman Zou provided valuable research assistance. Thank you to two anonymous reviewers and Chris Carothers, as well as audiences at the Cornell University Reppy Institute for Peace and Conflict Studies, Harvard University Fairbank Center for Chinese Studies Critical Issues Confronting China Series, and Lingnan University International Symposium on "Africa-China Relations in an Era of Uncertain Future" for feedback on earlier drafts. Thank you to Ching Kwan Lee for excellent editorial guidance. Finally, I dedicate this book to Jingwen Sun for her unwavering support and encouragement.

Global China

Ching Kwan Lee
University of California-Los Angeles

Ching Kwan Lee is professor of sociology at the University of California-Los Angeles. Her scholarly interests include political sociology, popular protests, labor, development, political economy, comparative ethnography, China, Hong Kong, East Asia and the Global South. She is the author of three multiple award-winning monographs on contemporary China: Gender and the South China Miracle: Two Worlds of Factory Women (1998), Against the Law: Labor Protests in China's Rustbelt and Sunbelt (2007), and The Specter of Global China: Politics, Labor and Foreign Investment in Africa (2017). Her co-edited volumes include Take Back Our Future: an Eventful Sociology of Hong Kong's Umbrella Movement (2019) and The Social Question in the 21st Century: A Global View (2019).

About the Series

The Cambridge Elements series Global China showcases thematic, region- or country-specific studies on China's multifaceted global engagements and impacts. Each title, written by a leading scholar of the subject matter at hand, combines a succinct, comprehensive and up-to-date overview of the debates in the scholarly literature with original analysis and a clear argument. Featuring cutting edge scholarship on arguably one of the most important and controversial developments in the 21st century, the Global China Elements series will advance a new direction of China scholarship that expands China Studies beyond China's territorial boundaries.

Cambridge Elements ≡

Global China

Elements in the Series